THE ENIGMA OF CRYSTALS

Margaret H Beveridge

Love to all.

MINERVA PRESS
LONDON
MIAMI RIO DE JANEIRO DELHI

THE ENIGMA OF CRYSTALS

ISBN 0 75411 311 6

First Published 2000 by
MINERVA PRESS
315–317 Regent Street
London W1R 7YB

Printed in Great Britain for Minerva Press

THE ENIGMA OF CRYSTALS

With Love To all.

Telling in tales, myths and legends
What came first, what things followed
From one to another, before and after,
Ending in laughter, and tears and delight,
Making you see all things with insight.

With love to Neil, Matthew and Martin

Contents

Crystal

Rainbows you miss,
Until you see how crystal
Brings them back for you to hold.
Place flowers within,
And you've attained gold.

Flickering, listening to your song,
Take heart, crystal carries love –
Love undefiled, unmitigated bliss.
Yet the thought of it growing
Still brings a sight to see.

Crystal, crystal, you are so to me
A similar beautiful thought for all.
Water latent, bringing light
That never failing delivers delight,
Sight of all, best thought of thee.

Crystal wishes for all to bind,
Hope eternal crystallising lore.
Happiness to assert crystal anon.
Your long life is crystal clear.
Everything on Earth is crystal, dear.

Drifting

Tired of wandering,
Weary of heart,
Lonely for direction,
Fearful for a start!

Preoccupation sinful?
Confused and rejected,
Wondering, wandering,
Which path, which hand?

Never standing all alone,
Never confident to try.
Happiness has fled because
Doubt came walking in.

Just to take the easy way?
Or be persuaded, changed and moulded?
Or let things drift – the easy way,
And sleep the passing, painful hours?

Memory bogs at interpretation,
Stillness and peace are what I seek,
Heartbreak is not a welcome thought,
To seek and then to find.

As a Child

Sitting upon my Grannie's lap
Was safe and warm as we sat.
She hummed tae me and rocked me well.
She told me of the tales of old,
When she was a young lass, I suppose.
Many tales were told afore the fire was oot,
For she parried wi' past and future too.
Yet always her eyes were bright and shining,
With the exciting telling of these stories.
The sadness when time came for her parents to go,
The wonderful time getting married after.
'Now always remember,' she said abruptly,
'There's more afore ye than any past.'
I assured her hastily I would recall.
Many years have sweet memories.
Sadness appears but not for long,
If you remember
There's more ahead, than past,
To appear to you always.

The Idler

The figure walked steadily down from the mountain top,
Down where trees were covered with spring fair,
Where, beneath, the river dappled and birds sang quietly.
So came the Idler with his violin to play all lays
That, from his face, carried him to a world enchanted.
From the hills above another man observed.
Who was he, this youth who played so sweetly?
But he never dared to move for the music was unearthly.
There was eventually a pause in the playing
And the man moved below but, as a wild animal,
The other heard movement and disappeared.
Who was this player who understood all around
Yet moved swiftly, hearing his tread?
The man looked eagerly but 'twas in vain –
All around was empty of he who played.

That evening the man, in the village pub,
Tried to find knowledge to use
Of what he'd seen, just anything,
But all he learned was some folk stayed in outlying cottages –
It might be one there, and made do with that.
Searching when one's heart is sore
Is a puzzling thing.

So next day he went to cottages advised,
For, having lost his wife, this man ached
To discover what could give him peace.
Up by on the hills as daybreak was formed,
He heard what he longed for – the tune giving peace.
Stood still and saw, within, a youth idly playing
The songs unavailed but lovingly conceived.

The youth casually stopped playing. The man waited,
Finally calling, 'Please, don't stop!'
The youth looked up, said, 'Why? What is the matter?'
The man wrung his hands. 'I lost my wife,
But your playing gives peace.'
This began uninterrupted playing.
The man could discern feelings – angry, sad and despairing,
Which finally turned into the love in tune
And he felt he was healed inside.

The youth said, 'Well, that's all! Must go.'
He looked surprised as the man thanked him,
Saying kindly but finally,
'Don't worry or trouble. I just play from the heart.'

The man went away but never forgot
The music played from the heart.

The Lake

She sat still and pondered
On the days when she sauntered,
O'er the past days she'd wandered
Round the lake where she sat.
Of how she'd climbed the hills with ease,
Which surrounded a huckleberry's relax,
Watching with pleasure all things about to begin.
The lake restfully would see to that.
The ducks swam and were followed by swans
Who, as stately as ever, found wishes true by dawn.
The young mothers, happily with their own chicks,
Saw the regular feeding as a thing to enjoy.
Bushes around gave a measure of privacy
And, a couple in charge, a touch of humanity.
Young lovers came here to taste the fragility
Of affection not tested, but about to begin.
Seats ringed the lake, the swans and the hills
Which last were tested with excitement by young with young.
Its peacefulness like an old song which is newly sung.
It catered for necessity and seemed beauty crowned.
All were buying bread to feed the various birds.
Yet it was never a song with a dirge.
The old lady remembered in times passed by,
She did not walk unless her companion walked too.
She could remember the walks with her father –
How time sped by without a sigh.
It almost seemed as if the swans were the same.
She sat peacefully showing them to her children.
The only difference was one saved one's own bread.
'Why don't they come and get it?' her small children said.

Well, the family had disintegrated,
But the sun still stood high in the sky
And she noted with pleasure the ways girls did their hair.
The tiny cottage for the garden had an empty look
But more came provided, even bringing books.
She lifted her head at the shriek of a bus,
And concluded that that was to be improved.
The sun moved silently up in the sky.
The old lady quietly fell asleep.
Wakened by happy noise, gives a start
But, when the old lady awoke, all had changed.
The lake had turned a distinctive dark blue,
And looking up at all in the sky,
The moon stood out light, with stars going by.
And she, confused, murmured, 'I must have had a wee nap!'
And peered at the change within the lake,
Then gathered her bags knowing she should be at home.
'Martha,' she remonstrated, 'remember, you're not a young girl.'
She betook herself slowly along to her home.
She could never remember the lake so late
And said to herself, even the birds have gone to bed.
Arrived at her home, full of quiet memories,
But made a note first in her diary of life.

The Ball of Fluff

While in the garden,
A ball of fluff came by.
I watched fascinated as it floated
About the trees, the leaves, the bees,
Never stopping in its flight.

That ball of fluff came silently and slow,
Till I never guessed where it next would go.
It fondled the flowers, caressed the moss,
Where it was next I couldn't guess,
But then a wind blew it high in the sky.

In the sky it looked at home
And greeted the sun graciously,
Till it turned pink and blushed,
And fell to earth upon my lap,
Lying there exhausted, tickling,
But at last with doubtful glance, flew away.

I'll never know how it did so,
Never forget such eagerness.
But watching over the hillside,
It seemed to dip to me.
Now the sky is lonely without it!

The Fishing Boat

The fishing boat soughed and persisted,
Through frequent waves,
To a meeting ahead of those said to be
Those in certain command.
'She's going adrift away up to the rock!'
Shouted one and all.
For they feared for their lives –
With an inexperienced skipper,
They would not be long for this world.
'Trim the sails! Trim the sails!'
They shouted one and all.
'Remember to pass the rocks first,
On the way to the harbour.'

An angel passing heard their frantic cries
And bent to assist silently.
One heard relieved shouts,
'Harbour ahoy!' in frequent bouts.
Then quiet, realising they were home.
The angel passed, shaking his head,
For these men had resisted
The door to Paradise!
He only hoped they marked his help
That they were safely home.
So see the men, safe ashore,
Wondering how this was achieved.

Then one elderly chap admitted
He'd been saying his prayers constantly.
'There must have been an angel passing
To bring us all safely home.'
Many men passed the story
Around for their glory,
Warning their fellows not to count
On that angel being there,
To see them safely home.
More were trained to say their prayers
In any possible event,
And seek the help of the angel,
For every possible happening.

The Astronomer

Oh! It's nice to be the wife
Of an astronomer,
Who always keeps the sky so bright,
Pointing out the sun,
As if it were a wondrous sight!

It's nice to be the wife
Of an astronomer,
Who always knows what to do
If sunny blue turns into skies of grey,
Therefore knowing just what to say.

It's nice to be the wife
Of the astronomer!
If the kids have measles,
And you get it too,
He counts the spots, and cures the lot!

Grannie's Story

Well now, you must be knowing
Of a person you know full well,
Whose tales become a byword,
Whatever she had to tell,
Or foretell. 'A story?
For a Sunday Prayer?' she'd muse.
'How would it be if I told ye of
The Grace of God
And how I became acquainted?'
Our voices high, we agreed that nothing
Would be better than that for a Sunday.
'Well now,' her voice thrilled.
'You must understand,
It was as a young bride,
And in a small house,
That this happened to me.
It explains why one must help
One another, for others
Are not of the same intent.
This certain Sunday, became
A day of upheaval,
And started in this ilk.
A man, whom we know well
From television, rang the bell
Urgently, we thought as we ran.
There at the front door stood the man,
Whose appearance we well know.
He came inside hurriedly, with two others,
Who, he told us, were his brothers,
And started to seek through all the house
For what he said he'd lost.

Upstairs, downstairs and in the playroom,
Went he and his brothers.
"Everyone has it but me!" he cried,
And I heard his sigh.
"What is it you are seeking?"
I said in desperation,
For I got a-feared,
Having no one but only you children.
I was alone with him, as his brothers
Were searching high and low. Then he said,
"What do you see in the morning?
What do you see at night?
What's a daily occurrence to you?"
Then his eyes fell upon the circle of light
Above the front door
And, shakily, he said,
"Don't you realise you are blessed
Each morning, each night –
A sign that you're recognised?"
He asked to buy the golden glass
That made our hallway glow,
And promised he'd try
To live differently in the future.
Well, what would you do? For my eyes
Recognised a growing of light,
That we'd long taken for granted,
For most felt the light in their hearts.
I calmed him at last with the promise
That he could come on the morrow
And take it forth. He and the brothers
Thanked me and we made arrangements,
And he promised to come on the morrow.
So I was left a-wondering how and where
He had heard of my address, and why?

Thinking, I went down to the nursery
But, when playing with you
A game to amuse,
Was conscious of soft-footed noise
But, by the time I went up,
They and the glass had departed!
I felt thoroughly faint-hearted
But they had done as agreed.
Yet I could not understand
Why they'd come as thieves in the night.
Yet looking above the door
To a gaping great hole,
I felt thoroughly discontented!
Contacted the glazier next day to renew
What I thought could not be renewed.
He heard my story and looked grim.
"Do you not know," said he, "that you
Had the Almighty's Hand upon you?"
And though he replaced it,
I was a poor thing,
Thinking vainly of distractions!
But one day I came back from
Helping someone and fancied
That still small voice was home!
And so it was,
For when I awoke in the morning
The Grace of God Circle had returned!
I fell to my knees with relief.
It was sent, I believe,
That I'd understand this –
One never gets by taking!
Understand?
Then the difference in life is realised
And your help is never denied.'

She'd finished, but we boys had run upstairs,
Gazing open-mouthed at the Circle of Light.
Her story that day indeed bore fruit –
For we helped many others on the way.

Gardening with Rain

Oh, bother! Oh, blow! I thought by now it would go.
Watching the thermometer didn't work so.
Today, I had planned to go cut the grass,
But watching around 'twas determined to say no
And now, in the rain, I must again gather the weeds.

What welcomes the rain tho' it is a pain?
What grows inadvertently bypassing the weather?
I'm beginning to think a water garden is all
Or the fish pond which looks nice in all sorts of weather.
The trees are grand to stand up to it all.

Remember,
That's it! See a dovecote entire with doves,
And no weather interfere with your plot,
Plus trees that flower or stand up to the wind,
And you'll welcome rain falling but not interfere.
The arrangements made, you'll care not for the shower.

After all, we need rain
To give life to all this!

A Moment

A moment existed –
Should time keep grace
And evermore balance on the sea?

That moment existed
For love of thee
And time holding all enfold.

That moment existed
For sky, cloud and light,
That time discerned around.

That moment existed
During touch, sound and sorrow,
Taking time's baton of joy.

That moment existed
Through tear, fear till tomorrow,
Till time was agreed to peace.

Wood

Wood is an exciting method to feel.
One discovers the warmth in sculpture.
Measuring becomes a natural element,
Held by your hand so you may see
Discovered patterns, varied if possible.
Hold and see how emotion is cut
For what subject worked reveals.
How last means for ever!

Because of this, careful dealing
Surrounded by a constant revealing
And you pause, seeing discovery,
Loveliness natural.
Tire not, sculptor, much is left,
Imagination within woodlight,
Purpose with song alway.
Thou hold what has always been loved.

When finished satisfactorily,
Sit and lose time
O'er what you have achieved in art.
For I wish I could turn into words
What you can in wood.

My Mother Said

When very young, my mother said to me,
'Do not drink coffee.'
Paused and continued,
'Unless in extremity.'
I did not know to what she referred
And, hot one time in summer,
I drank coffee with relief,
For it was soft and warm
And made my head fall, on the shoulder
Of the lad beside.
As he kissed me, I knew
What my mother had meant,
All those years ago.

When not so young, my mother said,
Was I not thinking of marriage to flower?
So I admitted I would not be long,
Unless he took too long.
A few months after, my mother said,
Were we not thinking to enlarge our bower?
So I told her true, but inadequately,
That we would not be long alone.
Time after that seemed to take a whirl
And I said to my mother petulantly,
That this waiting was long –
To see her eyes filled with tears and she said,
'It's the fragrance of life.'

Now I am a mother, as she expected
But the twins God sent me are directed.
There are many times I wish I had her wisdom in store,
Answering just what needs to do.
Now it is that we are old and subjected,
But old couples find their knowledge needed,
And our lives together seem an old sweet song
Nor ever a moment does seem too long.

The Telephone Rings...

I lifted the receiver
Of the telephone that rang,
And the voice said anxiously,
'This is the World speaking.
Do you hear me true?'
I said quickly, 'Of course.
How are you?
It's quite a while
Since your voice was heard.
Do you have a message?'
Deep tones answered quietly,
'Now, don't be afraid
But I'm going to bed early tonight
So all will be dark apart
From the sounds you will recognise.
All right? Goodnight.'
I stood standing with the phone,
Waiting for sound about to begin,
Listening hard.
Then the music started,
Though I could not answer that!
I began to dream visions –
Buttercups and snowdrops,
One could smell were near.
Then the crashing of seas always around.
Thunder made known,
But kitchen smells faint.
I even dreamt of my favourite saint.
The telephone felt hot,
As hot as the sun,
And a shaft of sunlight went over me.

The variety of snows
Were made patently clear,
And the drip of water outside the tap.
A voice suddenly said, 'Okay! Goodbye from me!'
I went along into my bed.
Yet, as I went carelessly,
Saw pink fishes flying,
The green beech tree.
The birds unassuming
Sang in harmony,
And bees buzzed through the clouds above.
I learnt the private name
Of the World was Elsinore.
Now dusk had gathered
With the scent of flowers.
My head drooped on my pillow
And I fell just fast asleep.

Great Uncle Cornelius

As children, the figure of great import,
He not only had once been a soldier,
But told many tales to sooth or laugh.
When he entered, all smiled to look forward
To a world of excitement and joy, brought to our reality,
Of getting through our chores to listen to this.
He knew and recalled what occurred when fairies abounded,
Told of feelings of flowers, not being weeds.
How that battle between had been extended.
How the sleeping princess had a secret life of love.
We could hardly wait for the next tale extended.
How Jack and Jill were ordinary till –
How and what the cat said after one thousand years –
Remember, they're allowed this gesture if they wait patiently.
Of Biblical stories we could look up for ourselves.
Of the entrance of thunder, how lightning calmed!
Sometimes we told our worries to him,
That grown-ups would not understand, but he laughed.
'Remember Scheherezade. She would always find a tale to fit!
Remember, one tale you loved, how you would no longer be
afraid.'
Mum and Dad looked anxious at times,
So we took up Scheherezade's cloak, and healed.
There are so few not aching for a story,
It's much better than if you worry –
Tales, sometimes old, or new, unfold –
The very reason why the soothsayers live.

How being alone is a gift,
If you can see the art of it.
Tales of reason, of compromise, there's one
Helps someone, whatever their guise.
As grown-ups now, we have not forgotten
How to assist many with this special way.

The day came when we learned
Great Uncle Cornelius died,
But he left a message for us,
'Remember all, that the tales I told
Were only a beginning for you to unfold.'
We looked at each other, with faces lightened,
And slowly admitted we'd never forget his advice.

It was as if he'd never gone,
As we remembered every last song.
And that is still so, as we find stories
To find all solutions and explanations.

Old now, it makes our hearts light
That we comprehend all those that seek.

Child Story

One day, a little girl and boy
Set out to prove that fish had wings –
That they might be the birds that fly,
But really carrying wishes to all.

This little girl and boy met later,
And laughed together about what's fact.
'After all,' said he, 'A fish is fact and a bird can't be ignored.'
How young they'd been not to realise the wonder in child's eyes.

Again they met but he ignored her,
For she knew something of his past.
So, hiding sobs, she ran and told the birds of her distress.
Unknown to her he went fishing, explaining his unhappiness.

One day this little boy and girl
Left school together and surmised
How the birds gave comfort even to see.
The fishing was great he said, with no regret.

They're grown up now and say always
That the fish have wings indeed.
Now they're married and can be depended on
For stories magical for their offspring.

Remember always, if you feel blue,
That fish have wings for you
And you'll find your wish come true
As, of course, it was meant to do.

The Bookcase Mystery

The bookcase in the corner
Is very hard to find,
But when you reach the contents,
Well, they aren't half a bind.
Half of this to me is that
Bookcases spread out in each room
And, visiting the study, you find
All four sides of the room are easily filled.
Bedrooms are nothing, if
They do not contain selected contents to read.
The sad thing is that many people
Just don't see it so.
They happily say, 'I can remember
What I did on the fifth of November.'
But in my varied library
Are many more tales that tell more to me.
Some ancient books are not everyone's taste,
But it goes to my heart when they're passed.
For these old books, with messages,
Saw me through parts of life only guessed,
Carried hope within and sheer delight,
Seeing some opinions confirmed.
Everyone claims their favourites,
But living long distinguishes –
You have to keep your opinions wide,
Always knowing that one day you'll find
Secrets of the world to you.
Never totally discount,
When your book can show
Why you should have accomplished the other.
So you realise that each man's taste is not his brother's.

But words in themselves
Do gradually show
Their use is never a bother,
If it assists in knowing which
To turn to when you're in trouble.
A prayer never goes amiss –
It's how to find rest for your troubles!

The Horse and I

When I wandered o'er the hill in peace
Under a soft blue sky,
My horse wandered along gallantly,
And I started to dream on my descent
That once I was a warrior bold
Who defended many young and old.
Looked over this time and saw a castle of high degree.
My horse neighed loudly and I awoke,
My sword in hand but quite quietly.
We cantered by some cottages,
And the sky grew dark in night.
My horse decided I should away,
And moved forward carefully.
I've often dreamt of this time since,
For even the cottages had folk at the door.
Where had I been?
What had I seen?
Have often dreamt of being a warrior bold,
And bowed my head trying to understand.
For my horse told me it was time for home
And we hurried together to familiar things.
This dream comes to me often,
And cannot be forgot,
But it's always the same.
We ride happily together,
Yet, am never allowed to get off.

Pattern

Many circles divide into something live,
Directing the subjection until reflection.
Still unremitting toil is conceded.
Grandeur of mass instinctively subjected.
Purvey the sand here with all work upon it,
And travel in their space undelineated.
Particles massive and shape seductive,
Conveying the article to the before.
No word as small, within this shape,
Written familiars pass time for many.
Quarter it, halve it, even divide,
And you'll find a new path for you to guide.
Dark falls differently here, nary a star
Could echo response until by your hand.
Similar within the morning's light,
Advertising what indeed it holds,
For circle in magnitude is an awesome sight
For it never ends without beginning.

A Nightingale Sang

One day by the sea a nightingale sang,
And told me the news of the day,
As I passed along, the breakers beside,
Way into the countryside tide.

The news that it sang was bright and gay,
Looking forward to the Spring's say.
It lifted my heart with its song always,
For bright was dim in the sky to say.

It lifted my heart, my heart all ways.
It lifted my mind to say,
'Come along, little one, come down to the bay,
For we've got a lot to say before day.

Come to the ocean if you have a sore heart.
Come down and tell me all from the start.
With larks a-telling what won't be long,
We'll reach you with our song.'

And the nightingale sang to me,
'Meet that strife with fortitude.
Go under the stile with blithe heart.
Meet all moments to smile among.'

Always, in sadness, remember the nightingale sings
To all in difficulty to bring
A calm heart and a quiet mind.
We never forget this song all day long!

What Happened Next?

It's difficult to say what happened next
For happiness played through the air.
In understood mood, green led the way
In circles and trances with red intervening –
Midst lone hearts a-creeping.
Blue sky held flutterby of yellow and mellow,
Till orange clouds brought some sense to population.
Bonfires flickered, all over the lands,
To comfort those afraid of the dark,
Which produced such stars as had never been seen
To enter within this wonderful persuasion,
And slowly the voices began to sing.
To hum was magic with trebles divine,
Perpetrating magnitude for aft and by.
Birdsong sang true to warble with a sigh.
Camels produced their own turn of speed
While Man started off on unforeseen deeds.
For movement and mixture were all around,
Till the sea came in strongly with a leap and a bound,
And morning light developed around the sky,
And people slept thankfully, humming peacefully.

The Dream Cabin

In the softness of the night, where the wind is free,
We went to a masquerade dance to imagine all things –
Things that hitherto we had been scared to pass.
The music was pretty, the songsters were gay,
But the crowd of dancers took away all things
That, before unmasking, made us come away,
To be free of the bustle and trancing of others.
Skating home, that night, in bright moonlight
With landscape white as snow but the lack of masks
Was welcome. It was beautiful and made us feel alive.
Reaching our island welcomingly, saw it with new eyes.
For here lay the answer to trouble,
Without masks to shade around.
Tall pines and fir still lifted around
Our cabin, looking both east and west.
It's a wonderful thing to want to wake constantly,
For the sheer beauty of morning and night.
To make toffee in winter for all's delight,
Knowing apples reddened by our hearth.
Sit happily down on that rug, gently,
For it's paved the way to a wheen of years,
To purposefully wake at night to see
And hear your breathing regularly beside.
Christmas is wonderful too 'up back',
With no worries or questions from relatives.
How can you explain that at last you're free,
Sitting opposite to the one to whom you gave your heart?
Sometimes when it's snowing just reach to each other,
And my eyes reach his with love untold.

Nothing

Nothing care I for anything,
And nothing's what you'll get from me.
The garden's bright with light new flowers.
The sun is shining all day long.
The others have to listen to TV
But nothing grows if you don't see.
The nothing night in starlight celerity,
Asleep with memories isn't nothing.
The ache of love is not nothing.
You collect in surprising things.
If you collect sport you've got nothing,
Nothing to view along your shore,
But simply collect and that's what you'll do.
Morning, night and noon are something plus,
Daylight reaching, sunlight eventually.
Look up to the heavens for what to see there,
Look and star count all those that shine.
Your nothing is eternal, you'll understand.

One Candle

How many have whispered lies, instead of truth?
How many pretended and sought vengeance?
Whom now do we trust for evermore –
That passion might be moved from Thy sight,
That these parts are there to adore?

How many sing truth all their life?
Hold themselves as ones to be emulated?
Remember what was given for thee
And know understanding as performed.
Meet each other for evermore.

Wash away strident strife within this life.
Bring forward quiet peace to understand.
We could all be one, but are we one candle?
One candle lights the road for many.
One action good gives life to all.

Engaged

You're just engaged
And you feel, quite naturally,
That something like this
Never happened to anyone before,
Especially looking at that ring!

You're just engaged
And gaze at yourself continually,
But you're still you,
Except your heart sings exceptionally,
Thinking of thoughts quite true.

You're just engaged
And the thought is still unusual.
But his hair curls well,
And the thought of each other
Makes you think right out of this world.

You're just engaged
But you see at last
Your heart had the right idea.
In fact, you realise
That your two hearts make one for ever!

There are Things I Ought to be Doing

The man says firmly, 'You don't realise,
There are things I ought to be doing.
There's the garden true, to grow flowers for you,
But, taken along with my work singing songs,
There's the ultimate, later, of a day by the sea.
Will you be ready if I burst in?
There's my golf needing practice.
My cleaning the shoes – when last did I do it?
It's time I attended the "Converse Literature",
And gave stimulation with my view.
But you can't do it all. Look at the time on the clock!
Well, you can't do all, with eyes drooping with sleep.'

'Alec, I'm touched by your thinking of me
In the middle of all these things.
But what will you accomplish if you're having that bath,
Cutting your hair and all else?
Wait till tomorrow, you always say.
Do you think one day you'll accomplish growing wings?
Remember Alice's birthday next week,
And the party you promised to give.
You'll never forget when it took us five years
Getting back to normal, when you first said this.
I'm not denying it had its points, holidaying in France,
To help us to realise that everything is a dance.
But sitting in sunshine, timing the cook,
Wasn't quite getting on with our life.
For I'll never forget what we came back to,
And the bill from the vet for keeping the animals.
Can you really forget all that?'

All night long, they tossed and turned,
Trying who should do what till the morn.
But serving breakfast, she broke silence to say,
'Alec, I've got it. We'll move!
There's an island for sale off Scotland's domain.'
If we lived there, the things wouldn't need to be done!'

'It's a sensible alternative, I must say,
But what would we do with the car?'
She impatiently replied, 'Get a boat, silly!'
But he said, 'Interesting, but you've forgotten
There are things about which we ought to be doing.
You've forgotten today the car's in for tuning
And taking you to the shops would help all ways.
I'd come myself to help with the rush.'

'There are things I ought to be doing.
I joined a club for domestic economy,
And don't have troubles anymore.
But I missed the days when you'd think
Night meant day for my Alec.
It oftentimes makes me remember.'

'It's a boon to have peace and quiet at last,
Resigning from all these committees.
I just potter about, because
There is always something to avoid.
Looking back is sometimes looking forward!'

The Curiosity Shop

I was just a child when I first realised
That almost every town had its secrets to share.
Go up to town, along the wynds, you'd find the same –
A shop bearing shelves of the precious stuff
Which could colour each century if you looked around.
Sometimes it was best to go to one or t'other.
Sometimes going through shelves, found a delightful surprise.
What you desired depended on you,
And made your road decided for all time.
The owners were interesting too,
Some selling with a whirl.
Old books were possible to contact still,
Old paintings probable and meeting at last.
Old cutlery showed the art necessary.
Plates and lamps were a 'view halloo'.
Sometimes there were platefuls, containing
Precious jewels and gems straining.
One could imagine ladies a century or two ago…

Many curiosity shops have closed.
Quite a few paintings the family don't understand.
In many cases I am left with books.
In many cases just memory supplied –
To bring sometimes the past to the present
And colour your thoughts thinking –
What was, is possible once again.

Struthers

Struthers was not a lovable man
But he was a familiar one,
Making money in his own way.
He assumed it must make the day for all.
Of medium height with weighted back
And looks suspicious, he did his following well.
You need this? Go reach for the following to sell.
If Struthers is running it, you'll get a good deal.
No one realised that the toll of his years
Troubled him, as many, in due course of time.
Finally in his rest, he slept and awoke
To find Gabriel by his bed,
And was safely accompanied without distress to heaven.
There was naught to look for, no enterprise,
And he caught Gabriel viewing him with pity.
'You worked so hard you had no time to become a man,' he said.
'Yes, yes, but I have a balance in the bank,
Truly formidable,' he offered eagerly.
Gabriel said, 'One does not need money here
If one has led a good life and helped others.
Come I will assist you.'
Will Struthers admitted shamefully, 'Then
Dost not count my money?' incredulously.
But Gabriel had memories still and said, 'You helped
The young while still at school, why pause?'
And Struthers found himself imposed upon the past
And saw helping others to learn before deciding to stop.
'There was nowt in their success for me,' he said sulkily.
'Yet it all counts,' said Gabriel, 'These men went forward
Successfully.' And Will Struthers listened. 'Listen,' said Gabriel.
'It takes a long time to pass that last long mile.'

Of a sudden, Will Struthers eyes filled with tears.
'But that is my mother speaking mellowly,' he said shakenly.
'Yes,' said Gabriel. 'For she has never forgotten.
You never found another such,' he added abruptly.
'Never!' said Struthers. 'I tried,' he continued softly.

When familiars enter Heaven, Struthers is there.
He stands with his mother who now knows fair
He was no mistake and they smile happily
That many took life from them down there –
She explained much to Will Struthers in kind.
How good and bad can rescind there and be found
And lie upon peaceful thought always.
Light and music eternally for all to gain their wings!

Have told of one man
Yet many follow, with exactitude.

Awake One Night...

Last night, when I lay unsleeping,
Against the twinkle of stars,
Thought that it would be colourful
Thinking of the past, when it was wonderful.
Even now, the thought of your eyes made me smile,
And I floated, willingly, to the world we once knew.
The past, greeting with a smile, but unquestioningly,
It carried days that were hopeful –
All of the colours were pink.
How gay days were easy to lend.
The scenery that we saw, the good things to see.
How friends shared happiness gladly,
Only wanting to be close by us at the turn of the year.
Eyes alight, confidingly, and hands wanting to know
How help be attained?
The small children learning from this,
That time passed soundlessly around.
And even tho' my eyes were closed,
I knew because of this
My door was never closed.

I slept soundlessly!

The Long Road

Walking along a busy street in London,
I felt a child's hand within mine
And looking down saw eyes full of tears.
The crowd swiftly passed, roaring
In a mixture of ways. There was no reason, and noise
In this passing was power and the road retched.
Taking the child into a park nearby,
Reached a semblance of peace.
Coolness touched the brow and rested the passing.
We together eyed the other's problems
And uttered the words, 'Be still' to each other.
I a man, he a child, yet we felt each other searching
But, finding a seat together on the grass, rested as one.
The people who passed, walking, chattering, did not stop.
Suddenly the child put a bunch of wild flowers in my hot hand
And smelling this felt refreshed.
The sky now darkened with the dusk of entered knowledge.
Seeing this, I asked him what was his name.
'Christian,' he said. 'You would not laugh like those at school?'
Then he asked my name, so I said, 'Timothy. But you know?'
Christian said joyfully, 'We know each other.'
The band at the end of the park began, and we sang,
Sitting together and watching.
Red blooms, blue blooms, yellow blooms, orange blooms,
In between trees which had stood there many years.
I said, 'Christian. You are no longer afraid.'
And he said timidly, 'No. I must do what I have to do.'

I watched the small figure, but it did not falter
And Christian disappeared. It was I who felt dismayed
And berated myself for not knowing more of him.
I said softly, 'Christian!' and it was as though
He answered quietly. And I arose among the crowds
And dreamily made my way for home,
But never have lost Christian.

Future

The flowers which form in the air,
In lines to the answers foretold,
In brief moments of life, in calm,
The stroking whispers of the sun's passivity –
These are the moments sublime.
For these form a speech of indefinite form,
And tell of the passing by of love.
Renew all memory and reach to the planets,
To gaze upon time's anniversary there.
Ye all shall meet and with love admit,
To feel the grasses and the air,
To tell of wonders untold through duress.
Look upon one thing, then another.
Turn warily to gaze upon each other.
Look and see, believe what you may.
Caress thou, while life saunters through a future,
Passing clear to what lies beyond.

Remember This?

The day, the day searched for so long,
We knew not then of that sweet song,
That occurred when you sang of happiness.
The very sea stood back amazed,
How you felt quite dazed...
Curled upon the hillside near,
When the sky went through its repertoire –
Sometimes as blue as knowing you,
Sometimes it cried out, though grey, for all to say,
'Come on, you can tell the wind –
Forget this seed of doubt.'
Waiting still, amongst it all,
Saw the best when dawned the sky
To rest, with moon up too.
The stars colliding, so brilliant and bright,
The moon directing.
All this I saw, with real belief,
One could see the impossible could come true.
But, in this time you've lived, as few have lived
And loved, compared to being afraid!
Everyone speaks of ultimate desires for change.
But that night, I encompassed this –
Each blessing rose with a fond caress –
One's heart filled with song and joy,
To partner us in future ways.
When, at last, I looked up, looked to my lover's eyes,
And others looked at the ultimate sky,
And we knew that we'd never be alone,
That we'd been blessed for years,
To spread our news of happiness,
Among all attending here.

The Fantastic Telescope

Once a small boy, well up in learning,
Heard a tale of a telescope
Which could knock at past, present and future's door,
And admit the answers sore as shores,
That pictured troubles in those things,
But also the answers to these troubles.
The boy, first using, was puzzled indeed,
But, being him, generated an alliance.
You see, it's one thing to materialise,
But another to escape those sighs,
Seeing wonders unknown, but how
To bring back to tranquil triumph.
Question time, but tell how to get relief.
Dance with glee, yet understand,
How to amalgamate with advantages.
How to accept, when something new
Is shown in this kaleidoscope too.
He soon discovered the four corners of the universe
And comparisons not being denied!
Seeing multiplicity, soon enfolded
Regular viewing as a gift.
And understanding of present led
To further implications of facts.
It became a familiar sight to see,
Living in the present, but a present made more
By all mankind had known.
How attempts in the future
Would become normality.
He lived for the sights reflected on it all.
It did not cast age, except when he married,
But could woo strangers with the tales
He told to all around.

Snow, Snow, Snow

The snow, we knew once, emigrated
But secretly dreaded that it should go
Past mountain and glen, the property of man,
Where the changes in the seasons
Were collated, though marked.
Snow looked to the sun,
It gazed to the moon
To enquire what it should do.
It contacted auroras all over the world,
For helping understand its life with song.
Demanded any news should be commanded
But, after this, snow felt monstrously tired
And ached for the summer's assistance,
And this hope at last was heeded,
For it melted that summer,
For relief to all.
By the end of this story,
Happiness existed as never before,
For nestling in sunlight frequently,
The snow was seldom seen…

Laughter and song came along,
To the alliance that mattered,
As ordered by the seasons,
And snow found at last it was wanted.
Where else, demanded some,
Would they get their skiing?
Face it, the curling pond needed the ice.
So all was allowed graciously.
Snow is insatiable that it should be.

Summer

The hum of bees, the tingle of leaves,
The swoop of birds to their private nook,
The wind in your hair, the flowers there,
Up to the sea, twinkling, and then see a wave.
Live exaltingly! What covers all error?
Live to be and then to see,
Live for life entirely and happy song.
This day is followed by another,
But who can tell its prayers and sanction?
Who passes before sweet love to arrive?
Who can retain thy perfect gaiety?
Feel the murmur present with heart,
Reflect upon a land afloat to start.
Start many days bringing music more,
And end with Love's muse –
Asleep till the bliss of morn
With song round this.

The Ball and the Cymbal

The Tale of Fantasy Corbett and Paul Leander

Fantasy: That I with thee do constant be
The fortune in thy sway,
But found my understanding with thee.

Paul: Come with me and walk with me to see –
See the changes within garden surrounding.
Thou must vow to love and adore me
For there must never be another for thee.

Fantasy: It is stars you go to be, time's swallows.
But now with honey for one man apart
Through the window see others
Yet they mean naught to me.
Thy hand in mine as wished and found.

Paul: (draws her close by looking troubled)
Fantasy, my love, you know I have the nickname of Cymbal.
In truth, I confess to you my temper is my unruly member.
So I trust thee, never be afraid, my love.
In sorrowful times, I still answer as Cymbal.
My dear, do I still be one with thee?

Fantasy: Oh soft mind, depend upon my inner sight of thee.
Together in all, we'll be as one. List to the song.
My dearest one, depend
For I will nurture thee.
Caress me, my dear, and have no fear.
We are the one to each other, dear.

Paul: (thinking)
Embracing her is seen by many,
Caressing near one is near another.

Paul: Living by touch gives certainty.
Moving in a stilly night which is ne'er forgot.
Our two figures move as a vine, held eternally.

Narrator: You wonder sore what happened here
Yet the one stuck well to the other.
War was passed and two sons gave cheer.
Time was endangered here, yet none did fear,
Yet Fantasy lived well with the Cymbal Paul
For many years mild to his speculating,
Speculating how looms might light the garter,
Employing many people and persons to start
That wool was certain, pertain to warmth.
Many swore by them to swear nature's doom
And lived to see the result of their labours
And pass them to the next generation.

Desert

Serene nights –
Nights that make you agree,
That lend ability to touch –
Touch an August sky when dark.
Your heart lifts as a lark,
Your mind rising to that climb.

Resting upon the upward slopes
You never are bored by the crop
Of constellations, sharing
Your night of hope,
While you hold the rope.

Your night which wraps around,
Showing its prettiness.
It's a pity to sleep when stars drop,
Touches of light everywhere,
But eyes flutter with weariness,
And you slumber…

Waking in dawn to grasp
More than you ever saw last.
The sun is moving in colours galore,
Your night adds this with even more.
Stiffly you arise in breathtaking light.

Understatement

The top o' the day,
With weather so clear,
Under the cobblestones are the burdock leaves
Near us, asleep and dreaming.
Dock leaves bend conversationally,
'My dear, did you see the colour she wore?'
Dandelion came bursting into this light.
Angrily, she said, with her voice a-quiver,
'You know I've to stay this way till morning –
As pure yellow.'
The burdock leaves were all nonplussed.
Clover took a look at them all, snorted,
And grew two new leaves.
Thistle came marching in, with laughter aside,
That as she came along, little prickles
Burst out, 'Ee-aa! Ee-oo!'
Chickweed was the pride of the world,
Who often came, but to look beneath
The cobblestones, and move intensively...
But a periwinkle, in her sky,
Was always the first to attempt
To instigate romance.
But, she never made a bloomer,
Until one came forth steadily,
Under the cobblestones.

The Beginning

When Adam and Eve woke up one day,
The Almighty smiled and this is what He said,
'Come, children, show your worth –
But have a look at all I have made today.'
They looked and saw possible all they wanted
But paused every while to understand,
How fleeting birds became messengers
While animals stretched their limbs.
The rivers were populated by many fish.
The earth made necessary with its worms
And the sky wrapped colour around.
'Now,' said the Almighty. 'Sing vociferously.
That you and yours all be one with me.
Tell me your doubts that I may answer truly
What direction personal patterns may go.
Always leave a space in your minds to think of wonders untold,
Always pausing for worship, to sing as you go.
You live an eventual life renewed, not death.
For with life renewed, discover thy heart.
But seeking My Word is brought into Glory with you.
Remember your kindness is often the link stopping abandoning all,
With all as one we all gain forthwith.'

The Kirk Session

The Kirk Session met, worried faces on all,
To see and discuss how they might stimulate contributions.
To see all sitting, they comprehended many things –
One had a talent for this, and one for that,
But all brought their talents to see through the Kirk's bad 'season'.
There were times in a cold winter all were grateful for that.
This November was cold and grey, but duty brought ideas alive.
But before they were settled the organist asked,
'Do you not think, with a song competition due,
That much would be gained in seeking talent for singing?'
And added that it would be a grand way to gain
The hymns and songs we'd be glad to remember,
And added persuasively, 'All kirks around are taking a place.
When you think – what betters our sound?'
The Kirk Session felt a bit dumbfounded
And discussed what would and should be with verve.
Then Mr Donaldson said, 'You should hear my Nancy!'
And others at once claimed the same for their own.
'Well, well,' said the minister, Mr Lindsay,
'It all seems to have decided itself.
It should be a real pleasure to hear the old songs.'
He was silent a minute, then added,
'My cousin's family play regularly.
I'll be having a word with him later.'
The Session at this turned and shook hands
With the organist, thinking also to ask
If Miss Minns at the school would enter in the organisation.
Leaving that concluded, the memory is –
You couldn't go up or down in the streets
But you'd hear glad sounds ringing,
For the school entered competition with longing.

And all found themselves thinking, though November,
It was indeed a wonderful time!
Bypassing the hard work that had gone in the practising,
As one said to another, 'Man, it would be
Just an extra blessing if they won.'
From all this, they reached tranquillity
And finished as County Singers of the Year.
And as the New Year entered, were glad
All the young voices were here about them
And heard Mr Lindsay say a prayer for all.

The Tale of Mrs McTaggart and Mr Bloomer

Mrs McTaggart was a conscientious woman,
Who kept all to herself in the village of Shuman.
Mr Bloomer was that reliable sweep,
Whom we all hope to meet for cleaning complete.
One day, the date told Mrs McTaggart
That her cleaning would not be complete
Unless she invited the Sweep to take a seat.
Mr Bloomer set her heart at rest –
He would be here tomorrow, and do his best.
She was to await his arrival, and he
Would put all right, with her permission.
She agreed, with accents of relief,
To await his presence on the morrow.
The evening, in both homes, seemed very long,
And Mr Bloomer thought, Bah!
My feeling for the woman is strong!
And Mrs McTaggart tried to affect
Her potent responsibility!
Next day, at first, they were both quite correct,
But that morning's break, he was
On his knees, asking passionately,
And she admitted a surge of a similar emotion.
'But what are we to do?' she voiced at last.
'Everyone would laugh, as all nice is past.'

She sobbed quietly. 'Listen,' he said,
'Maria, I make you an offer.
If you come into the business,
And answer the phone,
Everyone would believe in that!'
So they arranged, during this
Tempestuous wooing.
She became a part of the Sweeping!
They'd have a honeymoon in London,
Where no one would guess…
But come back together, in happiness.

They did not even sell her cottage,
Hearing in London of a pair who'd fit.
But no one really knows,
In the village of Shuman,
Whether the name of the Sweep
Is McTaggart or Bloomer!

The Heat of the Happy

The heat is well felt this afternoon.
It's stifling hot this day soon
With blue skies above and the sun at the corner,
The summer is welcomed by the corn.
The sea has invented several waves more –
A bathing suit is welcomed all over the bay.
Ships have wandered afar with many.
Parasols are the thing for ladies,
Kites flying high for the boys to the skies.
Violet sky's the thing in this heat,
Soft violet clouds to come after.
Games with bowls for elderly souls;
Tennis for the young, playing briskly;
But top of the lot is the ice-cream shop –
They're waiting in rows way down the street.
Hotels are waiting to pamper all folk
Who come on a sunny day to Cullen Bay.

A Superior Breed

The turtle doves came tumbling –
A very superior breed, you see,
Tho' sweet and frail they be
With furrows' heritage pronouncing
That all is free to be.
Listening and saying, 'We only came in December
To see the night scented stock
And play by the garden of what came after
And wash swiftly within Lake Tangatore
And watch swans as they ride passing sore.'

The Spring bustles by expectantly,
For she comes to see what arrives,
And we nearly always give her a surprise.
All her inspecting is never directing.
By the shore of Lake Tangatore there be
Dim figures of the past –
Confucius passes by with Socrates, talking earnestly.
Venus and her maidens practise their steps beautifully.
There float animals too who've succeeded
In being the heart of their home.
Cat or dog, it matters little to be such –
They don't disturb the sun in its orb
Or eventide with too much adventure.
It's only here you realise time and adventure both
Take their part in your heart.

Wonder and Discovery

Wonder and Discovery looked into the night
Where Balance had held a redemption bright,
Where found could uplift to impossible,
Tidying across many minds desultory.
'Come,' voiced Wonder, 'here is discovery.
Some unheeded with our distress in mind.'
Gravely Discovery agreed they had seen unanimity
But unity held, given horizons of sea,
And sensible held within virtue a sight.
Both heard discussion of later time.
Both compared reduction in part,
To surprisedly admit a mermaid on that sea
Playing around with fish-life about.
'Oh!' said Wonder in admiration.
'Oh!' said Discovery with contemplation.
'Nothing can dispel our sightings within,
For this brings substance to our tale.'
And greatly comforted, smiled to each other
And waves danced with t'other merrily.

A Sign for Subject

With magic employed,
There is little impossible,
To keep a light heart,
Amidst deepest heartache.

With magic employed,
Among those dark silent hills,
The sun takes a bow,
With hope and happiness.

With magic employed,
The night was lit in moonlight,
That every sight was employed,
And every light displayed.

Hold your magic for ever,
Your hands with your heart,
Your sound with your sight,
That you feel right for ever.

With this sign for subject,
You need never despair,
Across personal sea of troubles.
They'll disappear as bubbles.

From this light from this sign,
Darkness floats in the air,
And contains secrets to behold,
But that magic remains as you.

Entailed

My life entailed, when I met you,
Bearing the oftentimes hither and thither –
Doing the cooking, ordering the sweep…
But oh! Sweet lover, when we did meet
That summer was about our feet.

My life entailed, when I met you,
Getting acquaint wi' two small sons.
Remember carrying them on your back?
But oh! Sweet lover, remember all winter,
When every branch was set a-twinkle?

My life entailed, when I met you,
Singing, listening, the whole day through!
The day, when dancing, we altered our pace,
But spring came with buds here and there to us.
That Grace was a-winking through all our dares.

My life entailed, when I met you,
The news of the stars as we went along.
How you showed us unknown summer glades.
How travelling far, you attained your desire.
That travel, so potent, for I still love you.

PC Peter Pottifer

1 – On the Beat

Large feet stepped firmly
Far down as the Pond,
Gazing at houses while he went around.
For in those houses dwelt his family,
Some living alone or with happiness blest.
They all had their problems, just as he
But many relied on Pottifer's beat.
Steadily he moved up to his box
And sighed with relief that he'd made it that far.
His box held necessities and a nice respite.
Then on his round again till he saw morning light.
Sometimes, he noticed what he'd rather not see.
Sometimes interrupted by those unknown,
But steadily went round his beat,
With his lips tightened as some on the scene,
But taking the time went into the Police Station
And you'd hardly recognise that face was so bright.
Moving forward to the Chief Inspector,
Made free with his past night's watching,
For much can be seen without record
And trusted, as he took pride in the smiles.
'You had no trouble with the new distillery?' he was asked.
'No sir. The new watchman was capable company.'
By which the Inspector took it he'd had a few words en route.
But another piece of the pattern slipped into shape.
They said, 'Good morning,' and left for home,
PC Pottifer smiling with relief.

Next night, true as said, the feet repeated the round,
Then suddenly heard his footsteps covered.
So, suddenly turning, saw a boy and a girl
Doing their best to go unheeded.
'Miss White!' he gasped. 'And you, Mr Black.
What are you doing at this time of night?'
To hear confused information from both.
Finally he said, 'Oh yes! It's quite clear to me.'
And took both for a meal, at last.
This was really the Police Station,
But the confused words had made him pause,
And had to listen to fourteen-year-olds' views
Of the situation. But as he knew
The parents, it did make sense
And was able to put right that running away –
That would not help the situation.
He took both home to find both houses
Lit with anticipation and fear.
Both parents thanked him and shook his hand,
And fathers both admitted having a hard time at work.
They were out of touch with their offspring.
The mothers said little, their eyes filled with tears,
But Peter Pottifer was satisfied
With his night's work, as the doors shut
Upon two families, whom he'd known for years.
Of course, it would mean extra explanation,
But 'God bless the result!' he murmured.

2 – London meets PC Pottifer

One day Pottifer was sent for by the Chief Inspector.
'You've done well, Pottifer,' said he. 'But now is the time
To look at further climes. Hampstead Heath
Needs your work as much as Edinburgh.
Are you game for what it entails?

It might take your work further,' said he.
Peter Pottifer, realising this would bring
A possible promotion not extended to many
Agreed to a post, similar, at Hampstead Heath.
Everything seemed to go quickly and so
It was not far long until he found himself on
The train, leading through strange fields.
Aghast at first by the noise, his lodgings assured,
He took his way to the Police Station that night
Which gave credence to every anticipation.
It was strange all around and the people were different
And PC Pottifer resolved to get a map.
His mother had said, 'When I lived with my aunt,
The streets of London were so busy,
But many years ago.' The quiet of Edinburgh
Made all about him strange and he resolved
To cure this failing by getting to know much,
By sometimes availing of days when he normally slept.
So, gradually, Pottifer became aware of much,
Of many things on the scene.
It was not only guarding houses near
But industry and shops and such like things.
The work it took to be easy with a neighbour!
Peter Pottifer, for a while, slept when he could.
Meeting Charlotte at the Policeman's Ball,
Her happy influence assisted him,
That it was not long before romance took a place,
Becoming Charlotte and Peter to each other always.

3 – Mr and Mrs Pottifer, retired

Peter Pottifer sat relaxed beside the sea,
Thinking how he and Charlotte
Had a lot to remember before really retiring.
Both held a sprinkling of grey in their locks.
But, he thought, it seems to suit Charlotte.

Their only son, Ian, was Chief Constable
And swapped gaily reminiscences that did not matter.
Both knew the advantage of that.
Hearing the garden gate squeak,
Looked up with interest, recognising
A neighbour from across the road,
The elderly man smiled and sat down beside him.
'You're Pottifer, aren't you? I wanted to ask
If you would join us on the Town Council?
Your wife already joined the Women's Guild
And it would be a substantial contribution to our little town.'
So Peter Pottifer, taken aback, agreed
And said he'd do what he could.
'By the way, sir,' said he. 'What is your name?'
'Smith,' said the other. 'You're ex-police?
So indeed was I, for we remember
What many now have forgot.
My wife will be so pleased!'
Picture Peter and Charlotte
Who, having dealt frequently with others,
Entering at last on a new life,
With memories shared, but comfortably,
In that little town.

My Muse

How to tell a Muse which way to go?
See, I tell all within my sailing boat:
My jewels near how to compose,
Mine own swift pace, alert to space and song,
My describing of varied property within –
Remembrance of much long past aglow,
Words that from some enter a song,
Exclamation from the heart unbelieved,
The vegetation that gives colour unto the clod.
Feelings of longing and guilt admit
But all these have an entrance to see.
The sea-of-youth, saying its mouth,
The sky that alters, the star that glitters,
The boredom heavy passed which promised
Height, light and surmise of much dawn.
Telling thee how mine own apart
Began to show all apaced beside.
How words flew differently in this –
Delicate flowerets admitted secretly.
The wind that blows was one alone,
The summer sun covered all in eternity,
The laughter shared in thy company,
The sorrow hesitant though thine,
The years broke to joy in thy content.
How looking at much paused as such
To gain virgin power that share,
Carry through many lands, so free,
And rest thy sweet head upon my heart.
Gracias, virgin, that thou art all mine
As we progress together as one.
Thank Thee verily for my Muse!

The Broom Moves

Whoever stole you from that bush of broom,
Cannot believe your happiness given,
With colour so bright to lighten apart,
To branches which follow in harmony.
Any bird is welcome at this store.
Anyone knows he is desired by me.
No one is sad when wind blows with me –
Thou'rt only letting me know as thee.

Before we entered thou moved to me,
And thy bright yellow is always unkempt.
So we hear your singing continually –
A bell through stream, a lamp through seam.
Wind trembles the seraphim of afar,
For heaven it is who have seen thee,
Of happiness wrought and happiness seen.

Those Walking By

Do you ever wonder at the man in the street?
Or the woman with him who warms instantly?
Everyone looks at these smiles similarly,
For they wish to be like alternately,
And make up the reasons for these delusions,
Giving man and wife such delight.
They'll wonder if we don't carouse as they,
They say, but find themselves laughing.
They'll tell their troubles to you but always end
How their ingenuity put all right in a trice.
These people, who smile industriously,
Know there are sorrows to bear, but admit it
Till those laughing increase and give more.
When you meet their children,
Already taught sorrow,
But have learnt as their parents have
To laugh and smile.

One old lady said reluctantly,
'It's you knowing how to cope with bothers.'
One very young person was congratulated
On his ability to meet the facts with equanimity.
One very tired young wife faced her future,
By sending for her neighbours to tea and cakes.

All know it's disastrous working for your life,
But illuminating if you know some who give credit for this.
Don't forget the 'upper crust',
Especially when thro' living and being,
They have to work harder,
To gain their release,
And still know the benefit of a smile.

There's never an end to those vivid tales.
Have the courage to climb these mountains
With a smile!

Norway's Fire

The inward spreading fire of a snow fantasia,
Which sparkles and cools to inspiration.
Norway's light stirred in many ways,
Stirring and struggling to show what all do say.
Waterfalls, rivers, with above the midnight sun
And great hills' reasons massive explained.
Their lakes ripple and trained
For those who activate this sight.
While winds progressing far through the night,
Winter spirits and moves to the sound.
Hear possible trolls sounding their love.
Folk dancing around all this to adore,
Prancing to all this with daily sound.
Horses and carts and goats, meandering,
Tell only the beginning of all about.
For many have lived but accomplished much more,
For Norway's fire creates in many lands.

Father Christmas

Father Christmas sat and pondered
Of who wanted what and who which – necessarily,
And whether a detour to get to there
Would speed results of some and help the other.
He knew that for some he mustn't be late
And of others who waited trustingly
And, as he had so far to go,
Wondered if starting two days early
Would bother them much?
But, in the end, he decided
To stick to routine
And, with mechanics polishing his sledge,
Said, as he said every year,
'This one will be the best.'
But this year with added certainty,
For the child who came after
Had been remembered and weather set fair.
Would he have cover for anxious hands?
Of course, he was hurrying just for them.
The special fairies who made the toys
Had worked day and night just for him.
Trying on his robe he found that it was slightly shorter,
Laughed and gave a big grin.
Infinite thoughts were assessed to give secrets to many.

Whoosh! The sleigh took off with stars leading
To every home in the world, speaking
As he rode, raising his whip for the reindeer.
To every country sang this:
'Hark the herald angels flying.
Mark time, I am on my way.
Hither all with smiles a-flying,
Watch that laughing dream tonight.'

In three days clear, he reached home
That he might sleep until New Year,
And his mouth smiled with satisfaction
Of the warmth that enfolded the globe.
Nothing wanted, for he had won
Every heart to him enfold.

Jonathan Allbright

Once the babe who was in my arms
Spelt truth out to me –
Just what his future would be.
'Now,' said he, 'I will tell you
What to know and understand.
Your face has gone white.
Can you really,' he said
Interestedly, 'reassure me
You are really all right?
Remember to take me to the shore
Anytime you're not what you oughter?
Well,' he continued, 'I am a genius
Who must experience everything.
I'd better tell you,' he said,
'How and where to begin.'
Regaining my voice, I said at last,
'This just cannot be true!'
But he reassured, temporarily,
That when he awoke in a while
He'd be back, though somewhat sedentary.

When he awoke and had his drink,
I asked, 'Do you know my address on the moon?'
And was met with bright eyes
As he said, 'No! Are we going there soon?'
So calmly I replied, 'I speak of the future
But the address is "2A, Cove, Moon",
For the moon is ideal for coves.'
He drew an inner gurgle of delight.

'Tell me more instantly. I need to know more.
Is there a shore with sea?'
Together we mixed up a line picture.
'The balance sounds possible,' he said gravely.
'This alternative gives much room for thought.
You could leave me up there for twenty-one years,' he offered.
'Then write and find out what I've discovered.'
Taken aback I frankly said, 'But wouldn't you miss us?'
To be greeted with, 'Mum. You're so sentimental!'
And I wished I had not told him.
But then it was time for tea and bath
So that was done with the utmost celerity
And I popped him into his bed.

Next day I greeted him with no further soliloquy
And started with, 'Once upon a time...'
When he protested saying, 'Don't be a bore.
Haven't you learnt yet that what's good for yesterday
Hasn't much point for tomorrow?'
And was greeted with quiet.

He's grown up now and is a fine astronomer,
But never forgets
'What's all right for today
Is no good for tomorrow.'

Song

Have you ever remembered
Your existence, when
Many things were past,
But you recollected when
They were your very heart,
And a hard thing to start?
Do you ever remember
How, passing these days,
They held a surprise like sun,
For you in their eyes?
Do you ever remember
How the past became a future,
And the muddle displayed
Was just the soul of it?
Do you ever remember
People long gone that you loved?
For they created many a surprise.
For they taught you eternity,
How to realise dreams,
How not seeing how to reach for the stars –
Your apex of longing was well understood.
How the birds in the skies,
Could fill your eyes extensively,
And bees hummed near,
As your heart awakes.

Do you ever give thought
To your trying anew
Something that was important to you?
How garnering things past
Made you enter the future?
And your eyes sparkled tears
At the loss of your fears.
You'll never forget some things
Are there to recall.
Yet, you always hold past memories
With wings as they pass.
A start is a beginning,
Everyone knows that.
But never forget when it happens to you,
For you share together
In days and in years.
And you'll never question
Anyone's yields,
From their particular fields.

The Unknown Reaction

The unknown reaction is which road to take,
Not recognised often till courage apprehends
That skill may reach unprecedented light,
And time could pause throughout this ilk.
Courage and forward – do not delay this lay,
Recognise satisfaction can be a hard competition.

But always remember what brought you to this –
The hard road, but conquered till all is bliss.
Not many flowers upon your way, just weeds
Extolling their strength. Yet caress eyes and see
Another way forward – more work in it for me.
Yet here rise up as dreamers pertain
And suddenly agree it's worth turning
To a fire chosen with personal joy –
Sometimes the obvious, or scale different heights
And your muse is content, whichever.
Your moment of peace can be disturbed.
Raise these eyes to what you seek
For the skies have many ways to break
That unknown ecstasy which gives you rest,
Pausing then, observing the way on –
Hedge sparrows upon this road,
Briar roses in country airs,
Attend the music of this allure.
You have found your way.

Confusion at the Sunray Pub

The well adorned, bedecked pub
Was a tea merchant's dream, for it contained
Many teas entrained as bottles of wine.
Usually, it was the norm with men drinking beer,
Until the day Norman said, 'I want a change.
Give me a cup of tea to taste.
My mother lived on it, you know, until ninety-seven.'
In front of beer-drinking colleagues,
Got his cup, while they looked on interestedly.
'Aye, aye,' said he, smacking his lips.
'That's the stuff!' And asked for another.
So everyone there, to join the fun,
Had cups of tea as well as beer.
'You know,' said Mr McTavish, the owner,
'This would make money advertised
As the place to fit even ladies' taste.'
And the company chorused, 'That's right!'
That pub at Sunray is well known for care,
And girlfriends were taken to Sunray Dances,
With free tea offered enthusiastically.
Men with daughters looked hard at the suitor
Who did not know of the Sunray Pub,
Which catered for ladies as well.

William Blake

The progress of art grows slowly, entire,
As it dominates with your influence to survive,
Containing past years and future predetermination.
Where will visionaries go? To the hills for the free.

How then to present what exists
In palpable mystery concealed?
What, where and how in significant ways –
Colours touching, phantoms shown,
Follow magnitude full aside,
While we persuade our person beside.
Gracious mystery that shows
Calm to the peaceful thought.
One hour passes, another aside.
One sight is glad for the glow.
Fervent singing which comes forth inside
That thou long for the play of after time.
This lengthened article,
Sometimes is shadowed to be,
Sometimes a surprise,
Lying in everyone's eyes.

Conflict

The strife between seasons was marked,
For each had its way just like people…

Each season, they stand attended
That each one have time ascended.
The perusal of winter woken with spring
Coming to the peace of summer song,
All asking autumn what they do not understand.

Winter:	This year I shall be time's mood, The force inside of the tempest. The seas to me answer inevitably.
Spring:	Yet my longing days remember still. Cuckoo would be held welcome true. Growth lie in the land that hunger ne'er arrive.
Summer:	My attention is vast to persist the thinking days. Cuckoo is but a foil to me alway, For all understand light and growth are one.
Autumn:	All is to me the benison full grown of food. There is more to see on Earth to be. My shades end the beginning of much.
Winter:	Yet, all know to see they have not long. Cuckoo, with derisory tone, wait for thine hour When all that is much will come to me.
Spring:	Let all buds form within love for all around. Cuckoo! Thou art but one of many understandings. Small flowers peep, thou hast not long to stay.

Summer: In this the green leaf transpiring, others will follow.
Cuckoo! But now bring others in thy wake
For sun answer all that doubt believe true.

Winter: I break in to show the hardening of this,
The hunger rampant, the heavy cloud,
The glacier alongstream a phantom trial.

Spring: To answer a vibrant call comes this cuckoo!
My sun and stars be strange but bring desire.
The young are growing, earth and stream are part alive.
Let us agree in nature as all see us.

And all disagreement was disposed,
Nature will see alone with Him.

The Element Control

Mr Element, Fergus to his friends,
A respected citizen of Somerville,
The citizen to go to if you were in trouble,
Yet no one recognised his penchant for all things new.
How? was a word continually on his lips,
For he desired the capacity of friends able to deal
Frequently, and often, with their own work,
But he had yet to meet the machinations of old Martha Spratt
And couldn't understand how she'd been able
To help folk deal with the troubles in their stables.
He considered this and then, one day, suggested
That all she did was laugh and make a fresh cup of tea,
To find himself shouted down with many a frown.
'She may not know mathematics, but we tell you true,
She's the one to go to if you're in trouble.'
Friends spoke of troubles he had not known
And said, thankfully, 'She certainly helped with that.'
One successful businessman said,
'I could tell you, but I mustn't say how till she set me free.'
By now the interest of Fergus Element had risen to the sky
For she appeared to have gained to what he aspired in simple
'understanding'.
So he made up his mind to find out what her secret was,
And made an appointment for next day,
And gave himself away,
For only the curious made terms like that.
She even, at first, made up her mind to turn him down flat,
But she thought of those she'd helped and they were many,
And decided to see him at three o'clock.

Fergus Element, she remembered, had been a lonely boy,
Trying hard to keep up with his friends.
Anyway, she would see and maybe sort out his troubles.
She made herself ready for the interview at 3 p.m.
When Fergus was in sight of her door he could have turned and fled,
But he remembered the highly spoken words of his friends,
Knocked on the door and walked in.
Martha Spratt was a comfortable woman,
Who soon had the kettle on for tea.
Fergus found himself telling her how lonely he was –
Not complicated business affairs.
Suddenly, he found himself facing sparkling eyes on him
And a soothing voice saying unexpectedly,
'Fergus, you should be married, that you should learn
Troubles don't come with someone dear, near.'
'B-but,' said Fergus, to be told,
'I'll get my niece, Flora, to see to that.'
With the cup rattling in the saucer, Fergus said,
'Do you think – I wish – Flora would be grand.'
To be reassured with a pat on his shoulder
And old Martha saying, 'I'll tell her to be there Saturday.'
He tried to thank her but couldn't find the words
And wandered out by the woods instead.
The rest is past history, for Flora took over
And his face smiling was one among many others,
In the happy wee town of Somerville.
Besides he had an added distinction –
Married to a relation of old Martha Spratt.

When Crinolines were Ruffled

One time in the attic, one after another,
Were pictured the latest contests,
Among ladies of my past.
The way to wear through seven layers
Gives an added respect for the Victorian Age,
But no running about, all is stillness.
One painting I have of great-great-grandfather
Shows gentlemen had a freedom ladies did not know.
No wonder everyone thought of their male wander
Until, beginning to think, would I wish things so?
Modesty is desirable but –
You hesitate reasons for you never had it so –
Frocks so intent on covering old and young,
Frocks so severely looking for serenity,
Frocks so covered all held secretly.
What would occur in the personal turn and whirl
But had much effect upon serenity?
These pictures make children almost look severe,
It's hard to picture seven, eight, nine years.
If the fashion were ruffled, how felt the others,
Having difficulty with their undercarriage?

So look in mirrors,
And be grateful to see,
That figure of yours,
Is just plain comely to see!

Wonder

Mid summer storm and afterday light,
Called frequent hearts for keeping,
This one lengthened purpose,
For strengthened example.
Further stood longing with counterpoint,
Up in the sky when air was clear,
Flew the apostles to their liabilities
That man, with no more doubt,
Was held fast within confident relay.
Air was flying with self-controlled light,
Domained by clouds that flew fervently,
Reduced what would happen and when,
And wonder was born in fixed delight
In many hearts and many minds,
Whispering to some, calling clear to others,
That He was aborne was enough.
For happiness shot through longing
With times exalted granted clear,
So wonder existed with permission.

Metamorphosis

The Met Office tried to meet today,
And could not.
How to represent all clouds in the sky
Had gone with fond farewell.
The sun bloomed where they thought it not,
With moon a temporary distraction,
The stars found sound, used as extra light.
The cacophony of living sound was here!
That comets ran, full four abreast,
To find a robin in its nest!
The sky wore gold, abreast of all –
Anything less was not in call.
Rainbows called, and were found
Not needed.
The shooting stars about were maximus probus.
The planets were sent for,
To keep all in check.
So, in the Office, they gave up and concluded
That they had the means
Of wonderful weather for all –
Of wonderful feelings in half seen showers,
A passage of starting.
We'd had enough on earth
Of consistent bad weather.
They tried to describe how
But, with so much, found themselves baulked,
And charily went forth to see it all.
The sea adapted firmly, unsure at first,
That spray felt warm, sedating the rocks.
Inland, the excitement floated as a cloud,
And faces were brown, where 'twas never seen before.
The gardens – a simple mass of flowers.

True, people were astonished when
The roads too were covered with flowers,
But said, 'The horses and dogs
Be cared for at last!'
There's always room for the happy face –
Ain't it true?
This condition couldn't last, they said.
Yet, this was the condition
Our ancestors bequeathed.
A world of light and sound, they said decidedly.
What should change befall, they won't resist,
But their passage was now too entrenched,
Before they all saw sense.
Each man's passage has an introverted way
To see delight spread over land,
Sea and sky.
Goodbye!

Claim

Claim your respondent heart,
That you know which way to go.
No uncertain voice trips so.
Uncertain means are not for you.

This, all you mean to do.
Blush, for nothing comes quite so.
You do not present or feel.
All you desire is knowledge of mistake.

Only meeting him last night,
Yet only recognising right
And so, upon the hills alone,
You try to realise what set the tone.

He has fair hair, where you have black.
There is nothing difficult in that.
Irrelevantly, who else would seem so right?
When he walks along the shore,
You recognise him – heart's door.

What you show daily in your eyes,
You are very glad you waited
For the right time to be stated.

Time Aroused

Time
Is the cornucopia of realisation
That the home of time is in you,
That floating or reaching
May mean the same thing,
And eternal to some is external.
One repeats how long to realise
That some are better than others,
Dancing around the Eternal.
Some souls have seen little
Before purpose lights
The stillness of time
Within little purpose,
For it extends constantly.
'Coming.' 'Going.' 'On my way.'
Only mean you've decided
To let time decide
When you should have a rest,
And as you watch,
Something moulds in your vicinity,
To bring light
To many things.
So choose steady for direction,
Where you will sail.
All is really a part of you!

Other Ways

My sleep took me to uncharted lands,
Where people and things underwent long-forgotten ways.
Where time outlived light as it came as home.
Where seas of new beginnings existed –
They were the talk of the hour.
Where contentment assorted in peace,
And the laughter of sprites took one to eternity!
Where worry shook its presence off all,
And the joy of all time was seen,
Curing scented mystery intact.
Stopping occasionally on that great white way,
Silently woke to hope all would be remembered.
It seemed that all was bestowed through earth and sky,
But then another path took my heart other ways,
For uncharted waters take time to grasp.
When waking observed the squirrels playing,
Birds all singing near to the nest,
Insects flying with zest,
And with quiet began the silence asunder,
And stepped outside on that sunny morning,
Only quieted by the thought that further was possible,
That nothing had changed before asked.
One night shall go again yet never
And never would be the same.

The Unprejudiced Hour

This is the hour when all comes right,
The time you hope for and long to adore,
That you wait for no longer in disbelief,
For here it is with you.
The surprise jerks you from routine.
That hope you longed for
Really does come true eventually.
If it was not for this, you'd have no bliss.
No longings, you've wished for, would come true.
With everyone, it takes a different hour,
An hour that answers and replies
To everything in your life.
You wish to be pretty and now find you are,
To be young again, to find the answer for such.
Your longing for the moon's understanding is granted.
You wish for someone whose heart is always wise
And find, in this precious hour, private desires.
You hope to go where you would leave your heart,
And find every moment awake for the start.
All of a sudden, you sing merrily
And find youth returning for a start.
Memories and longings bring forth their hope
And much will be effortless, reaching your sky.
But remember a lost one to tell,
For you never dreamed this would come to pass,
But you're here with that longing undisguised.
Never think this is confined to thee.
Hope for it! Pray for it!
To come evermore.

You'd never believe this would happen to you,
But you will believe –
When it meets you open-armed,
For this is your hour unparalleled
In which new air breaks through.
It will come if you hold to your beliefs.
Let the forest and wood
Lie temporarily ahead.
With courage borne tidily
You'll pass to your hour with honours.
For in that brave hour
You remember fears that you've wept.
Remember the undecided hours
Replying all to you.
Wait peacefully for the furthest peak,
But it is for ever!

The Glad News

While you are a-singing,
While you are a-winging,
It comes to me at last
That you are the answer
To bright love's ideal,
That you and I shall be wed.
Oh, bonnie bell heather,
The bells of the future,
For no news as such
Gives import in style,
When you and I are wed.
No doubting's passing,
When dancing is dashing,
Such as me and my brave lad.
We'll dance to the test,
Filling everyone's creel,
And join in the morning's seal.
Great ones of the past
Will join us at last,
While great ones of the future
Hold us well in suture,
Till all dance and sing wi' us.
And after all, well sped for tomorrow,
Is gaiety among all of us
To dance with the best of us.
Church bells all ring
Blithely all over the town.
For after it's after, 'tis true,
Sleep safe in the future,
For days that are stormless
And steady for all,
And blessing the day we were wed.

Future as One Time

And in the sand
Where you and I
Traversed the sea
And followed the shore,
There do my lover and I
See the birth of morn
Ever laid by.
We heard the birds
And gazed at each other.
For together, my lover and I,
Were as one for ever.
My hand clasped yours,
Our eyes smiled as one
But our hearts soared
Recognising each other,
Knowing we had arrived
To future accepted.
Light garnered thought
And we discovered
Peace in mind hereafter.
Clouds swinging, a wind singing,
But blessed by sun
And both relaxed with relief.
No beginning, together, no end,
But as one for ever.
We ran joyfully,
Stretched within a vision
Of a line unparalleled in strength,
And a cortex of varied corners.

Though feared, we had confidence bestowed,
Seeing strange things we yet held as truth,
Involuntarily given sight of things to come
And the earth drawn to a close
Was all part of every man who lived,
A hint of confusion in what was recognised.
In this situation, the Heavens appeared
And their song for all with them.
Planets converged to a reality.
Stars in their multitude were frequent.
Peoples from all over the earth
Were recognised. Part accompanied
The sun, the moon – gold and silver to behold.
The many who were disorientated were calmed.
The seas were calmed, also,
And a great exhortation of people everywhere
Was expected for all upon earth and sky.
But a great gladness came to behold
And a certain peace welcomed all,
For prayer to all was now established
Upon land and sea, air and the heavenly host.
And the earth and the sky
And peoples throughout,
Seas and their multitude,
All had found desired peace,
And transgressed no more throughout.

The Many Minds Pass

The Roman scholars whose minds told one true,
Seeking one blade of grass to take forward remembrance,
Following the sky and Aurora's quiet tilt more,
Trembles the absent vine and swells the grape
In thy clear crystal showing most dear.
The moon rising clear, a step before crescent,
The old, old centre of a cypher contingent.
A day upon us has scarcely the length
For minds to discover these waters alternate
Which strangeness complied,
Without which beauty is not made perfect.
Many paths comprise a diligent mystery,
Sound determining the relaxation for many
To transmute varied anguish into ecstasy,
But quietness in person hold not vexation.
Strange times amongst a vast group
Yet, only after designs another
Is one world perfect not decided,
Where light assumes all power of light within.
It is enough we decide within form.
We can no longer cease to wonder
Another follows gracious on our way alway.

Sound Sense

Hear the song of the bird,
As it's getting near,
The fearless sound of the sea,
Mixed on the way with flowers untold.
Feel all hearts lift from the air,
Coming forth for it grows in time,
To wonders untold for lovers unexpected.
Climb up and further go free.
The answer to this is waiting for thee.
Music hastes all old forgotten lyres,
That many are echoed with a sigh –
That corporate multitude heartache.
What is life if forgotten it be?
Why no reply to predicament?
Yet further fly, definitions sweet.
An extra sleep to smell and see
As the clock sighs of itself.
Knowledge is born from this foretelling
And flows with glad universal trying of love.
For nothing is born without song
To last, love and yearn eternally.

How to Keep a Wave upon the Sand

One day Tobias sat
And looked upon the sea and asked just that.
For what made it come and go?
Simple thing to ask – how so?
As a child, he asked the old man near
But he, livid with horror, 'Do not ask what's here.'
And Tobias turned to another to get the answer clear.
'Young lady,' he asked, 'please tell what is the answer?'
The answer to what was an obvious thing and waited for a reply.
She answered, 'Why does aught occur?
If we knew, we'd be a seer.'
Muddled, the boy left without any answer.
He thought of the sea being drawn in
Till it made reason for rhythm on earth.
He thought of trees planted close
That they kept out air, sky and sea.
He came to the conclusion that fields around
Would not grow well, unless they had a sound.
Therefore, coming back to that sound of the sea,
He remembered the lullaby sung by his mother,
Even when she was tired and it was a bother.
How his eyes closed gratefully upon the sound,
And the sound sleep made him glad for tomorrow.
'So my own sea reaches the safe sand of tomorrow.'
He went back home restored.

The Dominant Angels

The Dominant Angels, when things first took shape,
Ordered the clouds to sweet amity,
And informed the sea when it would be most needed.
Their touch made the stars scatter around the world.
Their proximity veiled planets as required,
That, as the axis turned from stability to reality,
Everything moved as one.
The other angels, soft in virginity, but wise in sagacity,
Began to resent this, unless shared autonomy,
And the singing in Heaven began to deteriorate.
All was understood by the Almighty who said,
'Remember. I conduct. And sing with your hearts and minds.
For constant is he when raising My baton.'
Some tried to restrain, others filled the terrain,
But when commanded even the Dominant sang
And, having done duty, were no longer dominant.
Soon they found their strife sliding away.
Other angels, hearing, bawled lustily
But the Dominant Angels had had their day.
The only thing was, if you are in trouble,
The Dominant Angels are nominated to see all until right.
So both lots of angels are satisfied.
Both lots of angels smiled through time.
Never forget, if feeling fragile,
Just send for the Dominant Angels.

The Newly Weds

A bed, a table, a chair –
They told themselves that only that
Was what was needed,
As soon as they were able.
For they felt their youth
Would do away with extra goods,
For comfort together in their stable.
Then thinking, she said, we need a carpet.
But he agreed, for his bedroom cover was
An ancient carpet, with lots of wear.
But she spoke also, of cupboards for linen,
The choosing of a nice set of china
And his heart grew cold, for he knew
Everything possible had to be measurable.
The wee house was grand,
If she'd only ask the possible.
The house was even named 'Romance'!
But in this domesticity, felt heart-doubt
For nowt went in that was not a necessity.
He even volunteered, 'It is all right for a start.'
To be told firmly, 'It must be a proper start.'

That evening, he had a wonderful dream,
That the house was no longer a disaster.
For in this dream, he was going in the door
But nothing was there but a staircase.
He went upstairs, and saw that he entered now
Into two bedrooms, bathroom, and sitting room
At the back, with a kitchenette after this.

How had this been achieved? He rushed out
To see builders had built on a top floor.
Downstairs, under the stair, was even central heating.
The place was as bright as it could be.
True, the conservatory he'd wished for
Had become window boxes...
But was wholly complete for an entry.
Waking that day, said all things of himself,
And went straight to the builders yard.

Oh! It was a fine sight to see 'Romance' grow,
And conferred a certain distinction,
For folk round about were glad.

When they married next June,
It was well worth the waiting,
They'd only to put flowers in the window boxes.
When folk tried to congratulate, he'd only two words,
'Nothing's Impossible.' They knew it was true...
Even the lorries went slow, as they passed at night,
In a tribute to what could have been a disaster!

The Island of Cosmos

The island of Cosmos
Just happened to be,
Outside of our big front door.
A conjunction of stars enumerated,
To bring order out of the chaos.
It was so restful gazing at it,
Adjusting if necessary, combining in turn,
Told much to astronomers, helpful to amateurs,
Learning much of what could be supposed.
Apprentices thus were never short –
They had much to learn and withstand.
The senior astronomers always had something new –
A fascinating rhythm no less.
Most islands found have seas around,
But this was an island of persons,
Whose work was thus to learn of creation,
And the benefits therefrom ensued.
'The island' around was covered with green grass,
Looking towards the hills and mountains,
And peace lay upon these hills.
For a man, at last, could go there to think,
To return, in fact, with the answers.
If sluggish, the astronomer in charge would give
A lecture that provoked their understanding.
The astronomers inside forgot the time
Until a clock – that old-fashioned notion –
Was installed within the main rooms.
Then it was but a step for Cosmos to deem its need
And, at once, in a thunderstorm were the basic elements laid.

The word used was adjustment,
Which Cosmos could and would,
And senior thinkers doubled, as more came to see
How their country should deal with this autonomy.
Astronomers grew weary and ill at ease
Because, like others, they had their troubles,
Till arrangements were made, after three months work,
The rule was a holiday for them all in turn.
For it had been noticed, if not eased,
Their minds as expected closed for a rest.
So you went vertical back, better than ever.
Remember they had a lot to contend with.
The instrumental side was out of this world,
But it was definitely more satisfactory,
With time in Cosmos always adjusted.
And folk watched with company this wondrous lot,
But still had time to relax.

Pass

Wistfully, I wander thro' lands afar,
But certain sure must I realise,
The Beauty of One is a mystery to another.
Music mimics whole countries in this,
For basic sound is very far abound –
Abandoned beauty, a silent star sound.
Yet, floating meets Nature of its being,
Finding us about, grants us a sign.
Wonder! It is an opal! Yet stop! It is the moon!
Heralding the only thing we all comply –
Sun, stars, planets, rainbows, are all shared.
That all look aloft to seek their steer,
But none can discriminate any doubt.
We look gently at this world, and the next.
Wakefully, I lie surprised, with much to gain,
Waiting for the moment which comes when you're reborn.
Reborn in magnitude, above the sea's covert,
As it repairs and wears the land, it be
Softly returning the closing of mine eyes.
Truly, here is confidence to come anew, and breathe
The mirrored latitude of deep sighs.

The Fashion, 1998

The fashion this year is to recognise
Why your dear one always goes for this prize.
Long or short, fat or thin, he will monopolise
The colour in which you first met him.
So I move confidently to the pink scene.

'You know,' said the couturier, 'you might miss the score.
Cyclamen shading pink has become all the rage!
Small green slippers to tune, just think of that.
A hat that matches, or a mature cream?'
Forward to handbags in pink, to complete a dream.

'What of gloves?' I queried. 'Have they altered much this year?'
'Madame, madame!' she shrieked. 'Do not leave the scene!
Your glove matching slippers have to be seen!'
The mirror kindly mirrored me as taking ten years off,
And the blush of excitement was contained in my cheek.

With satisfaction gained, I asked, 'What of negligees?'
With gleaming eyes, she produced the latest in this guise!
Gauze, with blue and shining stars,
With shiny ribbons lacing a wonderful disguise!

So represent the fashion for my loved one,
Seen in this year, completely up to date!

Meeting

The quiet face looked into mine,
Which had to me a secret sign.
Before me was the silence of the night.
The eyes that opening looked at me
And saw the branches, saw the dappled rain,
The quivering mouth, thy locks with move entrain.
The small nose which moved all.
This was the head of which beloved.
The light which seek thy neck within my stance
And in the early morning thee did awake…
Looked at me and sighed to say,
'It is for thy sake all this entire.'
And grasped my hand which other held out to thee.

The secret of thy being speaking
Has often passed along with me,
Has taken loneliness from me.
For thou art with me as my guide.
We move as one always bypassed insight.

The Geese

One night looked up among the stars,
For the skein of geese was wheeling by,
And as they passed by cloud frequently
They flew in light periodically
And was entranced by light then dark.
Coming next day from the sea's pleasure,
Passed geese among winter wheat,
Not colourful within this weather,
Striking a longing for night
Indefinitely sighting.
The whisper came later in April
And looked at the arrival of geese
On their way with many unceasing
So saw all rest then take to the sky,
Flying close as they went by.
Since then in their elegance
Saw many nest while others took flight,
Their dark figures above were an awesome sight.
The young ones take flight as of yore
But see them off sadly that time every year.

Constant Laughter for Life

This tale is of one who was always wise.
If life was not light-hearted, she invented.
Picture the scene as the sun arises
And each nation laughs with joy.
Turn to your seer always around
For it is joyous throughout all years.
Can you imagine this, in each country,
Were maidens fair with laughter constant?
Kings could not bother nor someone other.
Everyone had Laetitia for joy
But everyone learnt, because of same,
Jupiter's mate was she ostensibly.
All watched the progress incessantly.
For these maidens fair all took to the air.
Nothing was impossible, such as love.
Though unimportant they could laugh –
Send warmth throughout any dominion cold,
Bring love to life which all did not realise.
Think of all beauteous flowers you know,
And they could tell them what to do!
For this generosity of maidens was many,
All over the globe – north, south, east and west –
The new world of high estimations in planet.
All this seems ideal until 2050 years,
When young men from the planets,
Came seeking for their brides.
The laughter and joy ceased for a while
Until in one country each a girl said, 'Why not?'
And righted the balance in the Cosmos.

Boys from unknown lands found homes
Giving news to further extremities.
Earth, sky, sea, planets and stars
Found to each other the perfect turn in life.

Wonderful to see, wonderful to be,
The new world's contribution
To love and life, song and understanding.
For all were happy, all years constant.

Folk Lore

Truffle, my Truffle, to the west of Tiree,
Where the faeries go dancing in sweet harmony.
Where doubt left a long time ago, leaving the peoples
To dance down to the sea. It's often told me
That mistakes made on purpose are the action
Of faeries in Scotland to stand up to the test,
Of wishing with horses on a purposeful note,
Brings forward a land contented, with zest.
When Truffle was wandering around Tiree,
She discovered the home of the faeries.
But, in this nest was Callum McReady,
A youth girded well for quality.
Truffle accorded a kiss to her love
And Callum McReady took the hand of his bride.
Truffle and Callum founded the first Scottish band
And their dances in moonlight are justly famous.
They have a choir made up of their offspring –
Catriona, Ivor and Fergus sound well.
If you're ever passing, remember
You're welcome to the west of Tiree.

The Post Office

Halfway down the street
Is the Post Office that you meet.
Outside, the exciting display
Of their red vans to deliver
Letters, cards, words of congratulation –
You never can tell what
A PO van might bring.
It might bring anything.
So keep your wonder when it's near.
You may be the one to receive
Joy without a tear!

Postmasters were invented
To have what you desire extended.
When they poke something out
It's hard to restrain that shout –
That parcel you have waited for
Is further joy when the time
Seems long, but still each day, later,
They will cater for wishes unabated.

The Musician

Almost everyone who plays an instrument
Will know this wishful story.
One day playing disinterestedly, you light up
And play better than you ever knew.
The violin, trumpet, or cello
Is born again to mellow chords.

It tells the tale that you have
Been waiting for in turn,
Reaches the very glory of what
Maybe you misunderstood,
For you play assertively, regularly,
With a difference in those chords.

Murmurs strength and follows height,
Until as if reaching a new firmament,
When doubting rings a brand new find.
Hopes and fears are charmed away,
While playing as if you can now say.

Audience alerted, many asserted on that day,
When instruments tell what to say,
And without doubt ring your bell,
That you can expel magically
And never forget that spell intact.

Twinkle

Take a pair of sparkling eyes
And see them arise.
Notice when they fall,
That lashes long unfold,
That your dancing feet extol.

For underneath those lovely eyes
Is a secret to surprise.
For beneath all this
Is a soft and dreamy thing
As those lips fall soft to you.

So we wander half amazed
In a very welcome daze,
That you and I are part,
And pearly teeth smile through
And together we are anew.

Sound Whispered Anew

A bird flying swift and unfettered,
Told a story of man's birth for you.
How an infant told a story,
That reached all but brought peace.
This bird a-flying got excited,
Yet pursued his energies,
That souls greeted him with joy,
That gave him the new note of arrival.
'Hearts,' he said, 'were in those smiles for all.'
So that no one ever be forgotten or left.
Telling so, believing so, the bird flew
Back to the others to gossip, eventually,
And then all knew silence.
Dreaming and seeming, undeterred flight
That would eventually
Take them to another's shore,
With memories that warmed their hearts,
At the thought of frequent starts.

Holiday Remembrance

Going my way with difficulty,
Lost my way untold.
A shop I passed sold me food,
And I retreated into a nearby wood.
Walking long the place seemed deep in mystery,
As the sky darkened I began to feel lost and frightened,
But this was leavened by the appearance
Of a small croft, though with no one there,
But it was sheltered and calm
And I made my way inside.
But I awoke in bright morning sun
And, looking at bushes, birds and bees,
Made breakfast happily,
And ventured to explore about.
Squirrels were upon the trees, and birds,
So I walked my way contentedly,
Looking at what lay around, buds and flowers.
First looking at the deer that crossed my path
And, at last, saw a bonfire burning steadily.
The woodman in charge could not believe in me
But, when I offered to make tea, gladly admitted me.
'My name is Jonas,' said he. 'And mine is Jocylin,' said I.
And so we were well acquainted, sharing our supplies.
'How did you come? Would you stay?' he asked eagerly.
We talked of all things quite happily.
Our plans soon became secure, for I have lived with Jonas now
For many years, that seem not many years.
He said comfortingly, 'You just needed a start
To be here at last with me.'
And I agreed, silently.

The Hour Uncertain

Rest within thy hesitant hour,
That hold thy positive or negative time.
Loving with heart the difficult strange pass,
We see actuality in reason's shadow,
Try here, try there, for intimate shade.
They told me that love did exist
For each in a pertinent way,
That coloured butterflies were born
But in a different way than corn.
So my lover should find my path
That, because of this, I am never alone
Within the indefinite obscure land.
The year my heart became alive
When months had uncanny witchery,
Turning and twisting till they to me in spring
Gave that blossom time away.
'Come again!' my heart said,
While I waited breathlessly –
The summer roses must be blooming now!
And it obeyed, only saying,
'See winter clear and entire,
Crystal clear in its spread.'

A Drop in the Ocean

A drop in the ocean swam by in the flow of the tide,
And that drop in the ocean felt inside,
The strange wandering must inevitably end.
The seas he had crossed, the river's bend,
But with courage, awake and mellow,
He followed circumference and bright insight.

A drop in the ocean is needed to flow along the spring tide.
A drop in the ocean is necessary to life
When that ocean approaches the heart of the matter.
Admit you are needed, every drop in the ocean,
That your mass is indeed many seeds
And your drops are never sad.

Find the drops in the Atlantic Ocean.
Find therefore your approach to countries,
Up to Scotland and find many drops around the Isles,
But they garner there with many stories to tell.
One drop makes another to curve like a slide,
And ends in happiness ever the days that abide.

The Highland Brigade

The blackbird is whistlin', my heart is a-twistin',
Joined by the boys of the Highland Brigade.
Squirrels are prancin', all things are a-dancin',
One to one as another breaks sound.

Hum while you tell me of river banks flowing.
Hum to the rhythm for songs to all people –
Hum to the animals, hum to the bees,
Hum to the birds asleep in the trees!

Join hands around those who tell all with song.
Reach your loved one before very long.
Stars bend down as you get it right,
And mountains and hills do seem such a sight.

Love softly gazing, you'll get it yet –
The way that takes you where dreamers go!
The sound of sweet music, alive in your minds.
How your song is one to reach to the skies!

The Waking Hour at Cullen Bay

Here among grey rocks, well met,
Further rocks and mosses around bend and set
And without pause came definite lie
Sea to cover as if adorn.
For, before we realise, it falls deep morn.
The thistles are grey, green company ahead
And along the sea's coming in is as lead.
The grasses grow vividly where they can,
With perchance an unknown flower!
This is a strange, waking sleep
With no wistful and wanting sun.
Ride slowly upon the path to dream,
Even if half moonlight filters glad sighs.
But soft! The birds awaken to sing,
To guide with strength this everlasting heart.
The hour is here. Silence as the sun
Makes known its presence sublime
And light trickles through this
As made known as morn's delight,
Singing as we multiply this perfect beam,
That sun has golden sand ahead!

Youth

A time when heart sings with questions.
A time when heart sings with the right suggestion.
A time when hand held, you've reached perfection.
When you can laugh at frequent correction,
Of a different selection.

When it's fun to take a different direction,
Still easy to discover that slight correction.
Interesting to find your way through another selection.
Till, finding a new song to sing, to perfection,
Until that kiss, the start, the beginning
Of a new communication for both.

Grow flowers, grow, from sheer appreciation.
All good is bye, all mystery selection.
For you tell me true that you love me,
And your nights are content with me.

Old Age and Compromise

A time for known surmise,
Accompanied by revelations,
By questions of youth tentatively perusing –
What, where and how best, intuitively,
Back where memory stretches to answer,
But find they've always got
Some secrets to analyse.

The fire burns and you are cosy together.
Happy both, if you can get on with your blether.
Content to eat scones and honey.
Content, also, if it turns sunny.
Good to hear news, even as a summary.
Dear, to be given that kiss willingly.

Helped get the hot bottle, that you sleep peacefully.
To share remembrance with you ceaselessly;
To enter into future plans extensively;
To be asked if I felt like you, anxiously;
To breathe a sigh of relief, courageously –
You're needed, wanted, and alive!

The Alternate Way

Dream that impossible dream
That you can see it come true –
A life without fear because of you.
Recognise the reason for this –
Knowledge is born because of a wish.
You really will look to the impossible dream,
Accomplished to the unseen,
But held with belief for tomorrow,
With unassailable delight, no sorrow.
Just working out a future for you,
Keeping further things to attain to,
Constructive emotion, not hollow,
Is a birth, rebirth for all.

Help is an unspoken reliance
Lest that help, born of defiance,
Sees the alternate way that doesn't need science –
The alternate way is making alliance.
Dream of regaining things our grandparents knew,
Of reaching others like you,
But garner the possible reason
Of making that dream through the season.
Fight an impossible wrongdoing
And be forced to admit
Things need not be an edict
Before others believe like you.
It's a way, a truth, a life!

Others have faltered, but recall
Even children are taught to apologise,
That your dream is not impossible
When it's taught to exist –
Existing to make wrongs right,
Desisting when it isn't right.
These things go to your head believing
You could attain your star!

Come along, come to view,
Things will be right for you,
But go on to assist and break fear,
Wherever it may subscribe.
Watch all who watch you,
To see what wasn't impossible at all.
Come with talents to unfold,
Things that were known of old,
That unattainable way,
For you.

The Minister of Keyes

The Minister, with difficulty,
Climbed what had once
Been as nothing to him.
For truth to tell, he was not young.
Now grown old to the ultimate design,
Standing on top of that rocky hill,
Thought over much of his life.
A noise in the trees made him look
And he saw a small boy looking eagerly at him.
The boy spoke, 'I don't know you.
Do you come here much?'
And the Minister thought,
Although walking a lot,
He did not know his flock.
This shock of surprise jerked a gasp from him,
As the boy spoke eagerly,
'My name is Erasmus,' conversationally.
'Thank you,' said the Minister.
'I don't see as many as before.'
'Well,' said Erasmus, 'it was jolly good to get here!'
The tears were not far from the Minister's eyes.
'I'd better see you home the rest of the way,'
Said Erasmus and he jumped down,
Saying lightly, 'My Grandpa is like you.'
So the Minister and the boy walked home together.
'I'm always there,' said Erasmus,
'If you want me. Goodbye.'
The old man walked home silently
And made a vow to see Erasmus
For he made him feel needed.
Later he thought, What of the others?
My friends are not so many.

It was noticed he spoke to the young,
Even going to the school for prayers,
But always by the Friday met Erasmus
Who in his turn, took his place
As the Minister of Keyes.

Clear Water

Drink into a future which is understanding.
Drink for a past which knew ecstasy.
Drink for kindness recognising being.
Drink to share wrath and open sharing.
Drink for happiness for the joy untold.
Is there no end?

It encompasses no end to endure.
Hidden thoughts made mild with delight included.
Behind us, past and future extolled.
Earth to sky and their beings untold,
Till venture to heaven and all the angels hold
And give the sign apart of what's held as compass.

A Man Like No Other

This is a strange silent man,
To whom the world has not been kind,
Whose battling through the years,
Has met with quiet tears.
Here it may describe the one you know
Going as from childhood to man's tether.
Yet we have been married long. Weather –
Weather is the time to call it,
Fickle announcement of passing change.
The muse in him is a fortunate music.
Yet knows his way to go, none else satisfies.
Loneliness is recognised, but passed as few can.
The stars in his skies are warped by many.
When walking to peace, it's like going through a wood,
While branches and forms take their place.
Here, somewhere, it is a form of instinct.
The gorse, the heather, the thorns, the weeds,
Begin to count what is rarely left out,
Coming at last to the shore,
Passing by waves with understanding.
Yet this man who goes by has more
In his soul than infinity.

Armageddon

When our last trumpet blares,
When everything is shared,
For the end of the world
Is in its bright shining tomorrow.
In this wonderful world,
There is much gladness to follow.
Every nation takes a bow and turns
Reversing all seasons with reason.
Everyone turns to their chosen path,
Albeit confusion in relief to follow.
One must remember all things that be
Have roots accordingly.
A fresh air to every country,
Fresh water as well, appropriately.
Difficult to place all things apace
Especially when they are there to fit.
Truly, the possible spectacle of time
Is magnificent when all are shaded in light.
Temper well your solicitude. Obey…

Heartbeat

Chappin' at the window,
Tappin' at the door,
Whirlin' doon tae see you,
For I love you sore.
Watchin' while you look out –
The brown bread or the white.
My arms around ye cuddlin'–
The things to tell tonight.
Pit the kettle on, ma luv,
Bring the teapot that ye chose.
Ma darlin', what to tell ye first!
Listen well while I tell thee all.

There he was and there she was
Lookin' in oor eyes thegither,
That we got marrit the next day.
And we're happy in the morning,
Well happy in the night,
But most of all when held within
Each other's arms at night.

Hope you feel so too,
That we were
The happiest people of all!

The Child at the Window

One morning, seeing it was fine,
Planned to get all messages for once in time,
And led me busily to the corner shop,
Which held a'thing needed by the street top.
Happily came back with bag bulging,
And hustled into my own home to sort,
Make a cup of coffee to celebrate,
But looked then to the window to deliberate.
There stood a child whose face was white
And in rags – made an awesome sight.
His hair was tousled, his eyes not bright,
As he called for help sightlessly.
What did I do? I brought him inside,
In pity for this boy in rags.
He came when told, eyes bright with tears,
And murmured, 'Food!' which I gave hastily
And urged him to tell past history.
A usual tale – he had run from family.
This usual tale told with tears and sobs.
'I ought not,' he kept saying, 'but it wasn't safe.
Had to go somewhere that understood my case.'
Sobbing too, I urged him to eat and promised
I'd give him a respite, for his sadness worried me,
And promised to do all to help that I could see.
To hear his weak voice shocked me.
He fell asleep and I looked at him tenderly,
That he could sleep in such a strange place as mine.

By high noon, with sun high in the sky,
My husband came in to shushing, slowly.
'What…?' he said, gazing at the wakened, wee child,
But the child backed away, quietly.
Me giving hot soup, begged to hear his tale.
At last, he admitted that he'd lied,
As no one knew really of his parentage,
Just repeating, 'They didn't love me,' many times.
So quietened, I gave my lunch to the child,
But this time saw it would not long be
Before he was a man and said instead, airily,
'There is a way to make dreams come true.
For all have suffered too.'
The child-man looked with hope as I divulged,
How writing made my dreams come true.
Every morning he came to me, ate and wrote extensively.
I gave him rest in the barn.
We talked, wrote and talked again
Till he had written what was like a spider's web
But lives at last in sureness bold.

His first book complained,
The second restored,
For he had found the way not to be old.
So if ever you see that 'child at the window',
Come forward even as a last resort.

Please!

The Controversy of 'Ah Micht Hae Kent'

Midst Aberdeen's contrast to all cities,
There in the middle stood Gran Kettles,
Who sighed at change, said she was near deranged
By modernisation of all things. If you tried to soothe,
You'd be blessed with her favourite sigh,
'Ah micht hae kent.' She went along saying,
Without sparing, aphorisms about new things,
Until in the middle, there was a pause,
And she confessed she'd got a sore toe,
And those near took her at last to the new hospital.
When the staff heard who was coming, many took time off,
But, as Dr Brown said, 'She's to go to bed.
Away with your blethers, you lot.'
So all was settled, and Gran Kettles
Was given a 'special tea' for her arrival.
For many days after, she was silent at the spectacle
Of 'What a grand tea they put up!'
So, in due course, her toe was lanced, under anaesthetic,
And she fell back blissfully.
'Ah niver kent things were like this,' wi' eyes a-poppin'.
She never said that awful moan 'Ah micht hae kent' once!
She took notice of nurses till they were coaxed,
And called her 'a fine old lady, forbye.'
Her interest in seeing was as much as being
One of the hospital patients to get well.
Her interest in the lovelife about her was not minded,
For they valued opinions so stable.
The doctors, relieved, let her stay on longer,
But the time came for her to go home.

Then they heard her indeed,
'Ah kent it couldn'a last long.' she sighed.
Yet never again did she bespoke all that was amok,
In the great city of Aberdeen.
The hospital became famous,
For the way it handled the patients,
And the happiness that it evoked.
And Gran Kettles changed her tune,
To go about saying, 'Ah'd niver be here but for them!'

My Mother Bade Me

My mother bade me bind my hair
And tied the ribbons on it,
Giving help, put my frock safe
And found her velvet cloak,
With handbag too, which matched.

It was strange to see me at last.
It was strange to be emerging,
My dark hair falling, welcoming,
Myself within that beauteous dress
Of pink with roses on it.

In this garb, I felt as I would be
Able to meet anyone on the street
Or within the party's home.
No longer was I all afraid,
But now one of the others.

My mother bade me do all this
In case I would behold –
What I did – that wonderful man
On whose shoulder I have leant ever since.
She told me be loving and giving always.

That I am proud to obey,
For life's pertinent tomorrows
That add these intense discretions.
I bade my daughter bind her hair
With pride this last Easter Day.

Professor Siskin

Professor Siskin was unique,
An invaluable treat –
When purveying secrets of finding.
Not just one nut but two,
Would be held in his beak,
And the young birds
Would follow to copy.
It was said that he was somewhat soppy,
But married Mrs Siskin soon after,
And the busyness of spring,
With nests full filled the hedge,
But Professor Siskin never stopped.
He had his students, then others to follow.
'Go up them steps,' he would shout,
'All is possible with a calm mind.'

One day, it was noticed by the birds
Professor Siskin hadn't eaten a thing.
When asked, he replied, 'I had an email
To say that my PhD had come through.'
So all other birds picked crumbs for his nest
So they could assist him having a rest.
Until, at midnight, he woke up at last
Murmuring consistently, 'PhDs won't stop the work!
Back to my old ways tomorrow.'
'Ask the Professor,' is often a sign of the birds
Eating their nuts with honours.
Look! There's one…
And another…
And another…

Seeking a New Life

I

When Alexander McAdam was off to his ship,
Folk gave him a great send off,
But Sandy was not long away,
When his ship foundered
On the South Sea isles.
He came home at long last,
A broken man who kept himself to himself.
Around the town the gossip was rife
Till a nurse arrived to help him with his strife.
Nurse Mackenzie was she,
Who broke the true news,
That he was little better than a cripple,
And many grey heads shook
At the news that was given,
And he such a great lad for this or for that,
And now hardly able
To take the air in the stable.
They little realised, though hardly able to rise,
That at twenty-five, a mind stirred in that body,
Thinking desperately what would keep him alive.
For he'd recognised his mind must take precedence.
Limping to the stable and gazing at the gables
Remembered how they provided a swing in the past.
One day he realised man had moved on a lot
And his eyes this night followed the stars.
True, he might limp, but his purpose was still there.
Shuffling indoors his bed was a welcome fire:
If he were to learn all the computer required,
He would sit, but his mind need not stop moving,
And he stood and thought and said,
'I could have lessons and go all over the stars.'

Drawing a breath, for his heart was wildly beating,
He would be no longer disabled –
The village postie noticed an increase,
For regular mail came and went to him,
And all Nurse Mackenzie could say or relay,
'He's reading a lot of information.'
They murmured good wishes and left.
But a strange, wee car was after observed
And though aching, Sandy learnt and complied.
He learnt programs to help with his stargazing
And after some months had satisfaction to hear
That the helper couldn't help any more.
The computer knowledge was up to him.
So, starry-eyed, a brave man began his work.
Realising as he did it, it might have been years
Before he, as a sailor, would have realised his dreams.
His programs at first were elementary
But he grudged the time not as he followed with patience
What he had comprised.
Nurse Mackenzie, not needed, went back to housework
With little to say except, 'He's fine.'
The curious were disappointed and gave him up
As a source of conversation.
Dr Smart was surprised.

II

Sandy McAdam now had arrived
Finding that distance and time were not,
Which was a good thing,
As he wanted to program various times,
To see what the stars were doing,
At particular times in the galaxy.

He worked on this solidly,
Till he realised what was needed,
Was the contact of a similar mind
And, with heart beating, started correspondence
With the famous astronomer Septimus White,
Who seemed quite excited at the extraordinary post,
But he ended with this, 'Why don't you put it in a book?
Few men realise what we go through.'
After getting this suggestion,
Sandy sat three days in contemplation.
Even Nurse Mackenzie noted the distinction
Between sitting at rest and with his mind busy.
On the fourth day, he spoke calmly but with direction,
'Do not be concerned, time is nothing to me.'
He had decided to write all his work.
That day was memorable for, like others,
He wrote non-stop for twenty-eight days.
Nurse Mackenzie, seeing that figure limp and aching,
Wondered if she should contact the doctor
But he just said, 'After this I deserve my bed!'
He slept uninterrupted, with relief,
For he had to admit it had been tiring telling his story,
Not complete without the addition of natural surmise.
One day, he awoke with hunger upon him
And, after breakfast, said casually, 'Any news?'
He was met with a torrent of speech –
How Septimus White had spoken of him
As one of the foremost thinkers
In the galaxy; how acceptance
Of his book had arrived
And all were agog for the outcome.
Sandy smiled at this, till his mail was brought in,
And realised what work it alone would make.

III

So he has Nurse Mackenzie to help
And, with her loving glance of agreement, relief.
There were letters from astronomers,
The letter from the publisher,
Letters from those who had suffered similarly,
But still asked for his advice.
After going through all this, he looked at
Gladys Mackenzie and suggested,
Being needful to the other,
Would she marry him?
The answer was affirmative and, when
Sandy felt her kiss upon his face,
He was a happy man.

He's old now but never forget his history,
For he's always spoken of with pride.
He is international by trying,
And let none forget that.

The Kiss

The kiss fluttered wantonly, like a cloud,
Another with it, lovingly.
They sorted one another out,
Filmed off all unspeakable doubt,
And landed with reason upon this face.

These kisses blushed pink, hardly moved,
Till they realised they were going to sleep.
Moved hastily around that face,
Which they found to their taste,
And vowed they must share part of the game.

'We've got to admit it,' said one,
'That we both do a loving job
And, that being so, should share about
Our talent within this operation,
Among others of our generation!'

'Practice makes perfect,' admitted the other.
'What we do today, others will follow.'
The cloud of exhaustion covered both
And they agreed with a yawn to go back to normal,
As the famed story of kisses ever wanton.

The Ascent of the Impossible

The first instinct of man
Is a means to arise.
Such was the thought
Of many a fervent lot
Of young, bold, fearless, inspired ones.
So give tender hearing to what was bought,
Always searching for what
Another may not do.

Two figures slipped out of a cottage at dawn,
Looked at each other and asked, 'Okay?'
And made for the impossible mountain,
Where they had been instructed not to go.
They were soon moving to their satisfaction
Up the grass and sod, trees and streams fast,
Upon this great though unfamiliar hill.
'To think,' breathed Titus, 'no one but us has been here before.'
'Congratulations', whispered Will. 'No one will
Disturb our folk; they're up at five.'
'Come', said Titus. 'We'll discover
If there is any reason – not by them.'
The base of the mountain was covered in trees
But soon stood apart
From all they recognised.
Strange flowers bloomed here apace
And to give confidence to the other,
They had a race.
They went at such a pace,
They did not see that here,
The hill went down
Into canyons filled with live secrets,
Who called to them in great delight.

'Young ones! Young ones!' they called,
As soon as in their sight.
'Come share our food for you to bite.'
'Keep running,' said Titus.
'This must be the secret
That they kept from us!'
Will nodded breathlessly.
'Come and look. It goes round here,' said he.
And so it was, for the hill
Opened so they could reach until
Walking, with tiredness, but still
Upon the top of that hill
And both sat down and rested.
'Gee,' said Titus. 'I could do with something to eat!'
'Golly,' said Will. 'You never said a truer word!'
And both fell silent, for inside
They felt guilty, not staying to bide.
Sitting upon the hill top, they at last
Were conscious of fruit going up to the top,
Drearily they went forward and filled up
With all the fruit that took them to the top.
'Congratulations,' they said as one man.
'We'll make it home, yet. Keep singing –
Keeps spirits high you know.'
And that is what anxious parents heard,
As they helped each other down to the ground.
Their parents stood and couldn't say a word,
Then they burst into tears, in their arms.
'Oh, Mum! Oh, Pop! We've been to the top!
We'll never wonder what's ahead
For now we really know!'
Their speaking grew blurred,
For they fell asleep,
Waking, each in their homes.
Yet Titus and Will, having achieved,
Never again thought to go away.
They were there to stay.

The Unstable Flower

Once when I walked,
Towards the sea,
Saw a mean, unstable flower,
That felt the footsteps instantly,
But held itself up tiredly.

Seeing that unstable flower,
Leant to it to adjust,
But of a sudden it held up,
That it be secure against the sea,
And though I'd passed I looked again,
For that flower moved with grace.
The grace held that unstable flower
Until it had had its hour,
Then stem limped and I saw,
That it had given its all,
But also, bending o'er, saw it had a bud.

Some time after, I walked along the shore,
The shore that gave it birth,
But alleluia! That bud was born
But not unstable, full and free,
Like tomorrow waking.

Prayer

In this crumpled leaf,
Recognise the wish to be with Thee.
Open my leaf softly,
That I may come to Thee,
And be a part of Thee.

In this distorted root,
Recognise my need for Thee.
Thus I begin, but some day
Thou wilt straighten me
And above will give praise to Thee.

In ugliness may start,
Yet one day Thou wilt show
Fruit grows evermore,
One upon another to see
Thou'rt nearer to me evermore.

In beauty adorned
Where Thou hast moved with me.
Showing me all for Thou I be,
And at last revealed
And our triumph sealed.